Redneck Spirituality
—Book Three—

Redneck Spirituality

Book One

Book Two

Combined books 1 & 2

Now—Book Three

The Courage of a Butterfly

An autobiographical novel

Based on the author's life

Written under the author's full name

Edmond E. Frank

Redneck Spirituality

—Book Three—

Enlightened Redneck Thoughts from the Pot

By
E. Egorhh Frank
"Coach Egorhh"

Copyright 2019
By Edmond E. Frank
All rights reserved.
No part of this book may be reproduced
by any means or in any form without
the express permission of the author.

ISBN 978-1-7327328-9-6

Table of Contents

Dedication
Epigraph
Acknowledgments
A Warning About This Book
Introduction
Terms of Accountability

Part 1—*The Spiritual Laws*

1   The Laws (39)

Part 2—*About Life*

12   Positive—Negative
14   Semantic Fantasies
16   Shit Down His Neck
18   The Shit You Dwell On
19   Believing is Seeing
20   Anal Attracts Assholes
21   Pissing on Ourselves
22   Perfectly Fucked Up
24   Perfection
25   Overdosed with Laxatives
26   Do You Have OPS Disease?
27   Self Esteem
28   Naked In Bullshit
29   Intimacy—In-to-me-see
30   Should-ing
31   I Am the Creator . . . Remember?
32   About the Sorriest Ass
34   Washing Off the Bullshit
35   Constipation
36   Explosive Diarrhea
37   Rude & Crude
38   Slinging Shit
39   Shame-ings and Should-ings
40   Falling Out of Integrity

41	Pull it Out
42	Not "Normal"
44	Getting Real
46	The MO Game
48	Hung-Up

Part 3—*Relationships*

52	I Am the Creator.
55	Perfect Love
56	Wanted: One Honest Woman
58	Shit Comes of Being Nourished
60	Shit in an Ice Cream Cone
61	Hi Ho Silver. . . .
62	The Game of Control
64	I've Touched Them
66	Picking Scabs
67	A Taste of Honey
68	A Fart in the Car
70	Monogamy by Choice
72	Getting It off Your Chest
74	Real Men & Cretins
77	Soul Mates
78	Of Controlling Women—and Scars
81	Control Is a Fallacy
82	Change is Scary
84	Trust a Snake?
86	Commitment Is a Fallacy

Part 4—*Sex*

89	More than Inches
90	By the Cock
91	"O" as in mOan
92	Garden Hose Sex
93	E-gasms
94	Experiential Learning
96	Society, Sex, & Racial Inequality
99	Sex & Judgments
100	Puberty

101	A Truly Selfish Mistress
102	Willing to Die For
104	Man's Man vs. Gurley Man

Part 5 — *Religion & God — The Higher Power*

108	Backing Up
110	Jesus Died—
112	Suckling at the Cock of Religion
114	Organized Religion
116	One Heartbeat
118	The "Wrath" of God
120	God Doesn't do Diarrhea

Part 6 — *Stray Thoughts*

123	Stray Thoughts
124	Integrity vs. Morality
125	A Man Who Lies
	Skid Marks
126	Old Chinese Proverb?
	Pissing on Someone Else's Parade
127	About Psycho-babble
128	Taking Offense
129	Shit Happens
	War of Words
	Winds of Public Opinion
	Male Maturity
130	It's My Shit—and, You Can't Have It
	He-e-e-re's Y'r Sign
131	Add to Your Backbone
132	Crazy Asses
133	Fighting Over Shit
134	Something Physical—Something Mental
	That Is Unless . . .
135	Stinky Pants
	Suffering Fools
	Waxing
136	Validating Stinkin' Thinkin'
	Doin' It

137	Living the Truth
	Pink Paint
	The Peanist
138	Stinky Shit
	The Direction It's Pointed
139	About Honesty & Farts
	Bickering
140	Dating—The Thrill of the Kill
	Going To the Dogs—
	Take the High Road . . .
141	Ego Fucking
	Sex For Barter
142	Move On
143	Y'gotta Know . . .
144	Ed—It's My First Name
146	Another Persona Note

Part 7—*The Final Exercise*

149	The Final Exercise
151	About the Author

Dedication

There is a Spiritual Law that states: Everyone is just a mirror for us to see ourselves. It's true, y'know.

Those things we see in someone else that we find just stink—well, it is really our own shit that we smell. If it wasn't in us, we couldn't even see it—or smell it—in them.

Truth is, whatever is in our face is a gift from the creator. The more obnoxious that gift, the greater is our opportunity to evolve and grow as a person, or as a species. It gives us a chance to see it, smell it, equate it, and then to change it in ourselves.

Only by owning it, and those feelings we have about it, can we change and grow. Some of the most beautiful flowers, are nurtured in shit.

*** Blaming others—well, that just stinks!***

*** So . . . I say to all those who have shit on me in my life,***

"THANKS!"

At the *least,* you have taught me not to stand under your big smelly ass crack. And, at the *most,* you have shown me how not to be that raunchy asshole I once was—that it is just as much a choice to be a *victim*, as it is *victimizer*. But that a much better choice, is *not to play the game of control—to just be loving.*

I dedicate this book to you.

Epigraph

There are those who will come to this game
to sit in the bleachers and observe.
And there are those who come to play—
down there, on the field of life.
So it has been with the first two books of this series.
Some read and observe and gather information,
seldom to be lived.
Others do the work—
search their hearts, answer the questions,
and do the exercises.
With those first two books,
the field was one of nice green grass—
and for some, grass stains.
But as always happens in life, it has rained since then.
This field is now muddy.
Consider: You know you are playing life the most—
when you are playing in the mud.
Hell, every child knows that.
So let that inner child free
and play this game with me.
There is great joy—and fun—
in discovering yourself.

Coach Egorhh

Acknowledgments

To the Sin City writers meet-up group for all their great critiques. And to Bobby Daniels Graphics, who did the excellent work on the cover.

Thanks go to Dee Ann Leger for her excellent editing.

It was great to have such supportive people behind my efforts in putting out this work. Couldn't have done it without cha . . .

Thank you, thank you!

Egorhh

A Warning About This Book

If you haven't read books One or Two, this is going to come across as INTENSE. That is why this warning—

This book operates from the standpoint of *"what is—just is."* When it comes to the question of morals, it ignores them. You see, the truth about morals is that they are only the judgments of a sanctimonious mind. It is the same with good and evil—right and wrong. If you are a staunch member of the "Moral Majority," you may not like this book

Do you really want someone wiping the shit from between their ears—*their judgments*—off onto you? I don't, and this book won't. But the thing about the moral majority, is that anyone below you in the pecking order, is just there to serve as your toilet paper—to wipe your judgments off onto. And no one wants to look to those above. Is it any wonder that many will dislike what is written here, and disagree with fervor.

If this is who you are—if you actually like someone else telling you what is moral—then DON'T READ THIS BOOK. You probably won't like it. Then again, it just may open up your mind.

What this book is about is what is truth, what is loving, and what works in a functional life. For most "normal" folks, it will fly contrary to much of what you may believe is the truth in life. That said, let's get on with the business of weeding out those who WON'T handle this well. Notice the word is WON'T, it is not CAN'T—

If you consider yourself a religious person YOU MAY OBJECT to what is written here—with pious passion. Don't get your BOWELS IN AN UPROAR by reading it.

If you find yourself offended by these words DON'T READ THIS BOOK. Outside of someone physically attacking you, there is no need or real cause to be offended. It is the response of a victim-thinking mind, bent on making itself *right*. Truth is, it is your soul telling you that you need to read this. The next lesson your soul gives, will not be so gentle. Those soul lessons that mean change in your life will *never* feel good.

But if you find yourself intrigued—if the nitty-gritty redneck realities of life interest you—then this book was written JUST FOR YOU.

Yes, I'm *talking my shit* here. But don't make the mistake that what I'm saying, is not the truth. The theme of this book is about "SHIT." I feel that it is only appropriate since shit is something few of us want to admit we do. And we all find it uncomfortable—even embarrassing—if those around us should happen to catch a whiff of ours.

And yet, it is the end product of what has nourished our bodies—naturally a part of just being alive. Those in the animal kingdom accept it with grace. But we humans—with us, it is definitely an *issue*.

Our quandary with it is *because,* we are sentient—we are thinking animals. But when what we think are the rules of life, are not the truth—when we base our responsibilities in life on lies—then the shit that comes out of our minds really does stink. We shit from both ends. This comes about by accepting the things we are taught as being the truth, without doing our own thinking.

There is one especially odorous lie—one that will burn and sting your eyes just from the stench. The lie I'm talking about here is simply the belief that we are not the responsible party—that we don't create our own lives—that other people *do it to us.* We—most of us—believe that lie simply because it allows us to blame our shit—and the stink of our own life's creations—on someone or something else.

With animals, the world around them is just that: the world. With us sentient, thinking human animals, our world is comprised of how we choose to view everything—our perceptions. If our belief is that we are responsible for ourselves, and our lives, then we believe Law number One: *I am the Creator*. With Spiritual Laws being the truth, there is no untrue mind-shit stinking-up our life.

Think about it: when you are getting blamed for the problems in someone else's life—and especially for their mean-spirited feeling—then you are witness to the stinky shit in their thinking. You now know the truth behind what it takes to be an asshole.

So, let's take it beyond the ass crack of someone else's mind—to the ass-crack of your own. This book is also about life, and this life—remember—is a spiritual experience, *all of it*. Can you now see how most of us have been *taught* to stink it up by the lies in our thinking—and how those lies have resulted in that extra asshole—the one that empties out what is between your ears every time you speak out in blame.

It's not your fault you've believed, and lived your life according to those lies. Most have been passed down—taught—by our parents for untold generations. And then there are our religions: much of what religions teach has nothing to do with truth or responsibility.

Face it, religions don't make you the responsible party in the creation of your life—God gives you all the good shit, while Satan makes you do all the bad. And your significant-other is responsible whenever you're not happy. Where is your responsibility in any of it?

Hopefully, this book will expose those lies by following the stink, and—taking it even further—will expose you to the truth. Along the way, you will find an occasional breath of clean air in the discussions about Life's Truths—the laws. Not all of them—just a few. And then there is the fact that this outhouse is OUTSIDE—outside the rules and regulations of polite society.

So it is I'll warn you one last time. This book may be seen as offensive to the delicate feelings of ladies—or gentleman. Likely, they will only see it as RUDE. But then, that is about looking through the eyes of a judgmental mind. But make NO mistake:

IT IS CRUDE!

It is as crude as I can make it. Sometime what it takes is a real stench to get some folk's attention. Just remember: LIFE—*all of it*—and even this book, is a spiritual experience. That is because of who and what we are, and who and what God is. That is what this book series has been endeavoring to tell you.

Introduction

This is a bathroom reader—a toilet paper book, if you will. It doesn't tell any particular story. There is no hero or heroine. And it doesn't much matter upon which page you choose to start. Still, your bathroom operates under one hard and fast Law:

Shit always flows downhill.

So too, does life have one equally inviolable Law that you may not know:

I am the creator of my life.

It is my only responsibility. Its joys—its sorrows—***all*** are of my own choosing: ***all*** are of my own creation. And my feelings about it ***all***—especially—are ***all*** my own. Cleaning my ass is best done with toilet paper:

never with blame.

Break either of these rules, and life is guaranteed to get very slippery—and very stinky. And if you should run out of toilet paper,

blame is still not an option! What is—just is.

And what is—is that *you still have this book in your hands.* If that is the best purpose you have for it—*do it.*

In my previous books, *Redneck Spirituality—One and Two*, I mentioned that I hadn't painted any turds pink in an effort to make them more socially acceptable. They do discuss shit and turds—the unvarnished realities of life—but not to the extent that this Book Three does, not nearly so.

Those other books were written in recognition of the fact that the vast majority of people get their chicken nuggets at places like McDonald's. This book was written for you who see those chicken nuggets from a much different perspective, one where you first went out and killed the chicken—chopped its head off—experienced that carnality by seeing its body continue to flop around. And now that it has nourished your life, you're out here, in the outhouse, discussing it, with me. No worries, I can't see you—but hopefully you can.

If this thought is something your sensibilities don't want to deal with—then likely this book will be the same. Those first books were also a gift of true redneck spirituality, but were not nearly so deep. This one takes it on down to its crude reality, You've got it—to this redneck's throne in the out-house.

"SHIT"—This book is full of it—
THE GOOD SHIT!

If I substituted any other words for it, this book would not feel anything other than contrived. Poop, crap, dung, scat, feces, manure, excrement, dump, duce—no other word suffices. It is the perfect redneck word to build this book around. It is the first word most go to when life isn't going their way. If your life was perfect, you wouldn't be reading this book . . . now, would you?

Hey! All life is a real spiritual experience—even this—even shit. You will do yourself an injustice if you will not deal with the shit in your life. This book will aid you in that—if you are willing.

This elevator is going down. Are you ready to get on? Can you respect yourself, if you do not take the plunge? And No, there is no elevator in my outhouse. Even so, one has ever died in an elevator just because someone farted. Elevator or outhouse, the realities of life can be unpleasant. In reading this, you've gotta know: you will survive this book.

Still, like books one and two, this too,
is not a feelie-good workbook.

What feels good are those things that validate your current thought system. If something's stinkin' in your life, it can only be because something's stinkin' in your thinkin.' Changing it never feels good. You can read this book, you don't **have** to **do** the work. But the uncomfortable part—*the doing*—is required to deal with what stinks in your life.

This is *your* life. It is up to you if you want it to be real and honest—based on truth—or not. Unless you're vegetarian, you're probably going to eat those chicken nuggets anyway. And too, it's up to you how *awake* in life you want to be.

I don't give a shit.

And that is not about me, disrespecting you. It is about me, offering you a gift. A true gift carries no expectations—y'know?

This book is in-your-face and it will poke you in some soft and vulnerable places. That is not out of meanness on my part. If I'm not poking you where you feel it, then I'm missing the mark. You will only feel it in those places in your life that YOU know you need to change.

There are those who will shine. Is it possible they shine *because* they are *being* who they are, and don't give a shit about what others think? That would stand to reason—dontcha think?

But wait! What of those who don't give a shit about others at all. Could their light be at all attractive to those who do care? There have been many of them—and they do stand out—but they never shine.

And what of others who, like me, have seen the truth of their lives in the face of death? It certainly lit a fire under my butt—got me up and hopping. Fear no longer stops me from saying the truth of what I believe, or from letting it all hang out—pretty or not.

No one wants to be ugly. But no matter what one looks like, one cannot long be seen as ugly, if their energy is loving. The very best one can ever be in life, is when living consciously in the space of love—to let love guide their footsteps in stepping past their fears in life; loving themselves, and loving others, regardless of what the others think or do. That part may stink, but a smell is just a smell. What if it were pointing out something about you?.

It seems that those who make a mark in life, have two common attributes: They share themselves—their thoughts—with others, and they participate in life. That is: they tell you their truth, and they do their truth. But wait! Isn't that the basis of integrity?

Exactly! That is what leaves a mark in this world: integrity—and participating in life. But to make that mark shine requires love—love makes the difference between just leaving a mark, or leaving a *glowing* mark in history—being a guiding light for others.

Some might question: what about Hitler? He certainly left his mark—or stain—in history? Yikes! Could it be true? Was Hitler a man of integrity? Hitler the politician certainly was not. He lied his way to power—as it would seem many politicians do. But once in power, he did not care what others thought. What he believed, what he espoused, and what he had the balls to do . . . was it then all one and the same—integrity? Yes, it seems it was. But where was the light? Where was the love?

What about morality? Did Hitler have any morality? Not many would think so, nevertheless, morality is the "righteous" judgments of one's own mind. And in Hitler's mind, his integrity was no doubt very righteous. But the fact is, integrity does not always include love. And morality has nothing to do with integrity or love. Bottom line: *when one's "righteous judgments" run one's life there is seldom any room for love.*

Now, getting back to the original question . . . What does all this ramble mean about me, and writing, and telling you anything? It is just this: Yeah, I've got the balls! Yeah, I'm saying what I believe. Yeah, I'm doing what I say.

And yeah, I know I cannot help but leave a mark. The only question is, will that mark be uplifting—will it shine? Do I truly care about anyone but myself? Do I love? Or am I just afraid to die—without light—slipping into what many in this world fear is the blackness of an eternal night?

Hell, a shining mark—or a darkened skid stain? With this book . . . you decide. In the redneck reality and shit of this book, can you see the spirituality? Can you see truth? How about light—is there that love? Yes . . . you decide.

Only someone who is truly spiritual and loving will understand—and will see it in the concepts of this book. This book is about "shit," the bottom-line basis of what has nurtured humanity. Can you read a book like this using the eyes of love? Can you answer the questions and do the exercises without feeling it? This book is not about the author. It is about you. It is about getting "real."

You may have some harsh feelings about what I'm saying, and ignore me—now. But sometime—maybe—you will hear and remember: maybe at a time when you need to.

Terms of Accountability

There are certain terms used in calling us all to account—terms such as INTEGRITY, RESPECT, TRUST, ACCEPTANCE, and RESPONSIBILITY. Is it any wonder why in the "world of normal" such terms often seem to carry a slightly different meaning to everyone? Why everyone tends to *tweak* their meanings just a little to suit the needs of their own ego—kinda like, make themselves—and their behavior—"right."
And is it a wonder why one person's values may differ so greatly from another's?

But hell . . . who's perfect? Even so, I'll gladly share what those terms of accountability mean to me—define them—and be held accountable. Yet, such are things of aspiration. Staying in integrity with what we say we believe . . .

Well, integrity even at our best, is something we really only aim for. Occasionally, when we realize we're missing our mark, we have to stop and take a new bead on things: re-affirm who we are, what we believe, and what we are about, then go about life anew. Personally, I think what really matters is the heights to which we aim.

INTEGRITY: What one feels in one's heart—what one says in their words—and what one does by their action, are all *one and the same*. And, integrity must incorporate a sense of *intention and courage*. One must have the courage to share with others what is in one's heart. Others always know where they stand with someone of high integrity.—That's *"high," because integrity is a term that is absolute, in a real world that is not.*

RESPECT is not something that need be earned. Nor is it a gift, for there are expectations. What it is, is something **loaned**—and loaned with generosity upon first meeting another person. What that person does with it—whether they have interest lost, or interest gained—is determined by the way that person displays integrity. To respect another is the recognize in them, the very best of what is within ourselves when we are being our greatest, in integrity with the spirit of who we all are when connected with what is of our highest essence inside.

TRUST is something earned by the strength of one's integrity. Yet integrity is something that permeates ones whole life. It is not something that can be missing in only one small part of it. If someone exhibits a clear lack of integrity, consistently and without any attempts to realign themselves, can they be trusted? Is it wise to hang around with someone you do not trust? Isn't it then a matter of your safety in life? Isn't this what good judgment is all about?

ACCEPTANCE of someone simply means you don't try to change them: It has nothing to do with whether they are someone you want to be around. Isn't it best to *accept* everyone . . . and *choose* carefully those with whom one wants to be around?

RESPONSIBILITY: Everyone is responsible only to the manner in which they live their own life. Is the energy with which one lives loving? Is one following the joys of their own heart? Staying in integrity with one's self and others, and having the courage to speak and live one's truth? The standards by which others live their own lives and what they think about ours, is none of our business, or responsibility. Those with similar standards will be attracted, the others . . . maybe not. Those who choose to feel abused by how others live, will be self-made victims. That is not the choice someone makes who lives with responsibility.

Truth is . . . we are all perfectly imperfect. When a responsible person steps out of integrity with others, he or she acknowledges it, and cleans up the mess. Yet sometimes it takes the other person, to point out when one is out of integrity. In that situation, a responsible person has the courage to let go of their need to be right, because what a responsible person values more, is truth.

PART ONE

The Spiritual Laws

The Truth of Life

The Spiritual Laws of Life

Book One had sixteen laws listed. Book Two, another ten (26). This book has thirteen more (39).

As to where they came from—there is always someone who insists on knowing the source of everything, and doesn't want to think for him or herself. Thinking that if someone else didn't say it—some egghead from the past—then it can't be true. I can't tell you who that egghead genius was, other than to say, I don't believe he/she *ever was*. I believe they were just other folks like me who didn't want to die, not knowing.

Socrates expressed the truth of it long ago:

"The unexamined life is not worth living."

Socrates paid with his life for speaking his truth. I have no wish to do the same. I don't claim to be the source—I believe God is.

So . . . to you astute people out there—take it up with God. If you'll look, you'll find Him/Her/It inside your heart.

I've searched these truths out over the last 25 years, and admit: I've not discovered them all. Some of those I have, I offer to you, as follows. I'm not preaching, just sharing this with you, a redneck who has looked. I expect that because you are reading this, you too, are looking. So it is with love that I can say this without prejudice: again, accept these laws or don't.

It is your life, not mine.

The Laws

#1—I am the Creator.

Most only take this to mean I create my own life. That is true. But to own it requires me to understand that there is nothing in my life that I have not had the deciding factor in creating. It is true, too, that all other Spiritual Laws presented here, are just aspects of this one. As you read through and comprehend the concepts in this book, you will get a sense of how this Law touches upon the infinite.

#2—Thoughts create.

Look around you. Everything our species ever created began as a thought in someone's mind. As for the rest, there is an order to the universe. One that speaks to sentience—to feeling, sensing, understanding, creating—like us, but much more. It is a "Higher Power" infinitely beyond what our religions can conceive.

#3—Thoughts are energy.

In being our own Creator, we choose in every second of life, the energy with which we are creating. It can only be one of two energies—the energy of *all that is love*, or the energy of *all* that is not love (fear).

#4—*The energy out, returns in kind.*

The energy of your every thought determines what comes to you in life—*love* or *fear*. This is that freedom of choice which is our greatest gift of all Creation. It is this choice which creates the path of our lives and the quality with which we walk.

#5—*The Universe always balances.*

With every sorrowful thing, there is the potential for an equal joy, yet we are the creators in our lives. There is equal joy to be found in every sorrowful event, *If* we will look for, *and* accept it. The truth is, it is we who have chosen the sorrow, and it is we who must seek and choose the joy. The potential for both exists in balance within the universe, and we are but a shift of mind away, requiring no more struggle than the acceptance of our next breath.

#6—*The energy of thoughts must flow*

Once taken in, the energy of fear stays and is the initial cause of all sickness *if* it is not felt, acknowledged, and then released. Even love energy must be released—given back out—in order to *flow*.

#7—*Along with being the creator comes responsibility: one cannot BE the Creator and play the blame game.*

One cannot *not* create. Each person must accept responsibility for the totality of creating their life, especially for all thoughts and feeling associated in that process. *Blame is the abdication of responsibility, the greatest of all Mankind's dysfunctional lies.*

#8—*The world is not "out there"—it is "in here."*

It is comprised of every thought, every belief, and every feeling you have. Your world is totally your responsibility because you are the only one who has the ability to respond—the ability to make it better or worse—loving or fearful. *Only you can change your mind.*

#9—*Others are but a mirror for us to see ourselves.*

What we don't like in others is but the reflection of what we don't like in ourselves. If it were not also within us, we could never see it in them.

#10—*The purpose of life is for those lessons.*

When we refuse the learning, the lessons will be presented again, more forcefully until we learn them—or die.

#11—*Self-esteem requires integrity—it is the respect of your soul.*

What our heart feels, what we think, say, and do—all must align as the same, and be coupled with the strength of intention to be in integrity. Integrity commands esteem.

#12—*Our lives are run primarily by our needs—then by our wants.*

As such, our lives are mostly run from an unconscious level. We all know what it is we want—few know what we need to have it. Needs are about the necessities—wants are about the quality.

#13—*Our life is our sole possession—and so it is for everyone.*

We, being the Creator, have all the say in creating our own life—no say in the creation of anyone else's. They are always free to be, say, or do whatever they want—without actual harm to others.

#14—*Change is the constant of the universe.*

Change is fearful. With everything we find fearful, change—the unknown—will be at its core. Fear? Fear is *not* a constant. It is a choice (Law #3). And sometimes, it is a barometer for change.

#15—*To create a functional life requires one to do one's own thinking.*

The beliefs passed down through the generations, as well as by our religions, are generally accepted as truth. Even when those "truths" serve us falsely, few have the courage to think for themselves. It takes great courage to think differently in the face of family and/or religion. Dysfunction will always come when living the lies passed down to you by others.

#16—*Controlling anything outside ourselves is a fallacy.*

We can only control another in as much as they will let us—or rather pretend to let us. And our world? See Law #8. Yes, we control our own world, because it lies within us.

#17—*The energy to which we hold fast is what runs our life.*

Mostly it happens from an unconscious level. This is why on the conscious level, forgiveness is so important to our souls. Forgiveness means, to let go of that energy.

#18—*Soul to soul pacts are made in the pre-existence.*

Each agrees to provide the lessons in life the other needs for the growth of their soul. Those people in your life who it seemed were especially mean—maybe you asked them to be. Was there a lesson from them that required them to be so?

#19—*We are quintessentially, beings of energy.*

Our energy affects that of the others around us. We cannot avoid it and are always attracted to those of like energy.

#20—*God the Creator—that Higher Power—infuses the energy of the whole universe.*

We are part of that energy—we each, are a part and piece of God.

#21—*Real love, once given, cannot be taken back.*

There are all kinds of interactions that are generally billed as "love"—lust, caring, companionship, even ownership. All that mislabeling notwithstanding, "real love" is an all-or-nothing gift, given without exceptions, expectations, or demands for anything in return. Real love begins with loving yourself. The love you hold within you—for you—*is* the love you give to another.

#22—*We can only feel our own feelings on a conscious level.*

Your love for another is a gift you give to you. The feelings—the energy—of others? That is felt at a higher unconscious part of our Soul: Our Soul comprises the total energy of our being—most of which is beyond the conscious. On this conscious level, you can only feel yourself loving them

#23—*All life happens right now—now is the only time there is for the living..*

The past is dead, and the future belongs to our dreams. We have only "the now!"

#24—*Whatever our thoughts dwell upon with energy, is what we are attracting into our lives right now*

It may be our fondest dream, or our worst nightmare. Some call this "The Law of Attraction." It s simply how we use our energy in the creation of our lives. Being actually a part of God (Law #20) we too, hold the power. Few realize it is an ongoing process—constantly using that power in the creation of our lives.

#25—*Your every word is an order to your soul:*

Thoughts create, and if you don't want them manifested into your life, then that thought, and especially every thought once spoken, must be consciously cancelled, *with passion.*

#26—Change requires truth.

One cannot change anything about one's thinking unless it is the truth about what one's heart wants. And one cannot change anything about one's life without first changing one's thinking. Change your mind—change your life. Pretending to accept someone else's thinking is to live a pretend life—never sustainable, always dysfunctional.

#27—Life—all of it—is a spiritual experience.

There is no part of life where God is not present, experiencing life with you.

#28—Those times when life is at its most chaotic, are the times of most opportunity.

Change happens most often during those times, because that very chaos gives you the reason to make that change in your thinking.

#29—Your soul is you—from the lowest to the highest of the energy of you.

We are beings of energy inhabiting this physical body. Very little of that energy is required to run this body, and even less, to run this consciousness. Most of that energy resides beyond what our consciousness can handle.

#30—Your soul is God—essentially made of the enigmatic substance of God.

God is infinite and our physical self has not the ability to know infinity—or that aspect of God other than through glimpses of it inside ourselves. God is everywhere and everything, but seeing God begins by looking within our self.

#31—You are God—a drop in the ocean of God—a part of, and the essence of it all.

Like DNA carries all aspects of our physical self within each of our cells, our soul carries all the aspects of God within it. And we are our soul—remember. Perhaps the 13th Century Persian poet, Rumi, said it better: *"You are not a drop in the ocean, you are the entire ocean in a drop."*

#32—There is no good or bad, right or wrong, it is all God.

Those things that only we can conceive of as having a beginning and an end—a duality—are about us and our judgmental minds. The mind of God has no beginning or end. (Law #30). In this world there is the energy of our thoughts, and ONLY in the energy of our judgmental thoughts, does there exist the energy of what is not love—fear. God has no fear.

#33—Everything that happens in your life, happens for your highest good.

Your soul orchestrates your life. And your soul *is* God—remember? Would God want anything less than the highest and best for *you*.?

#34—*The heart wants what the heart wants.*

As it is your soul directing your heart, this could also be stated: The soul seeks what the soul needs

#35—*We have absolute abundance, limited only by our belief in ourselves—in who we are—as God.*

If our needs—physically, mentally, or spiritually—are lacking, it is really our belief that is lacking. Abundance is the yardstick of our belief in our connection to source—our belief in God—our connection to oneness.

#36—*We cannot give what we don't have in abundance inside.*

To give away what we need for our own sustenance is to commit spiritual suicide—a martyr's knife to the heart of your soul. Worse than the simple lie of blame, it is an attempt to absolve yourself from responsibility in your own lack of belief, your failure in creating abundance. You are the Creator. As such, it is only your lack of belief in that as fact, that keeps you from absolute abundance.

#37—*Living is a conscious choice. Dying is also a choice—usually an unconscious one.*

We live our lives until we have either completed our purpose, or quit. Truly living requires courage. As for our purpose: we are an actual part and piece of God, y'know. Our purpose is often so grandiose as to be scary—should we ever live so well as to conceive it. Most people don't have the courage to aspire to it, and quit.

#38—*Our world is one of duality. Without duality we could not know love—or come to know God.*

Love is the bridge connecting us and God. It spans the abyss of all that is not love. It takes this experience here, of knowing what love is not, for our souls to know what love is. God is love—infinite love.

In our world of duality, there is black and white, hot and cold, sweet and sour, night and day---always a beginning and an end. Even our thinking runs in duality. There are things we think are good and things we think are bad. Then there are things we see as right and things we see as wrong—even though the truth is: there is only love and everything that is not love (law#3). *This is God's truth that points out the abyss between.*

It takes this world of duality for our souls to know god. All that is not love exists only in our own minds—only in this world. Man/Womankind need duality to exist on this plane—God does not.

#39—*If it is not love, it is a cry for love*

The energy must flow (law #6). It is the energy of our fear that pushes us to love—to God. If we let it flow.

PART TWO

About Life

What is—Just is

Did you come here to sit in the bleachers and observe?
Or do you intend to actually play in the game of life?
If you came to play, you will need a notebook—preferably a binder
type. If you aren't playing you may still find the show amusing,
but if that is all you want in life—

TURN ON THE TV AND WATCH A SIT-COM.

Positive—Negative

This too can be looked at as simply the judgmental shit from between someone's ears—yours, mine, or someone else's. In fact, the words don't mean shit because the concern lies in whether it is loving or not. And this concept may be a stretch for some. The truth often is.

It is ALL loving, if it advances who you are—gives you an opportunity to see the truth more clearly, and gives your soul an experience of it.

Where it is NOT loving lies in our actions in response—in the intent behind those actions. Is it loving or not?

Everything that happens to you in this life has been orchestrated by that Higher Power. That's right: your life is run according to your soul's needs—or, simply by and for your soul.

If your response is unloving—coming from your fears—your soul is merely giving you a lesson—one repeated until you learn to respond with love. And that, sometimes requires multiple takes.

I intended to make this book a down-'n-dirty set of concepts meant to get you to look at yourself, but now realize that for those who haven't experienced *Books One and Two*, this book would merely come off as me being negative.

Hard-nosed though it may be, in order to guide your perspective to be looking from the standpoint of truth—the laws—this book needs to be loving and I see it will be necessary to supply you with the

abbreviated laws to help you make sense of it all. You may read them in full in section one as needed.

This book will, therefore, be laid out like the workbooks One and Two of *Redneck Spirituality*. That is why the section preceding this one is on the laws and has been expanded to thirty-nine in total.

Laws:
8   The world is not "out there"—it is "in here."
3   Thoughts are energy.
10   The purpose of life is for those lessons.

Questions:
- Can you see how the shit that happens may not feel loving, but it is always nurturing to our souls?
- We've always been told that God gives us our freedom of choice. Can you see how it may be that our choice is in the energy with which we live and choose to respond?
- Do you see that it is us who label shit as positive or negative, good or bad—how we do it by using the judgments we have been taught by others? To look at it as loving or not loving—now that brings it home and makes it personal. Dontcha think?

Semantic Fantasies

What are we talking about here? Spiritual Laws? Life's Laws? Truisms? Whoa! *Truth? Does it matter?*

Yes, it does. What we're talking here, are simply those things that *always* hold true in life. Yes —*always*! Many have said that there is *always* an exception to the rule. They're thinking that they can *always* find one so that they can get by *without having to observe that truth.*

Our minds are powerful—the creative force of our lives. We have to be right. We will *make ourselves so.* No matter what insane fantasy we need to twist reality—the truth—into being, we will *make it so.* But this isn't Star Trek and you aren't Picard—*no matter what your fantasy.*

Like blame, exceptions to the truth, are another of the great dysfunctional lies of Humanity. Just like the creator made laws—physical laws—this universe must follow, so too did He/She/It make laws that life must follow. Disagree all you want, but if you want your life to work, *then,* SUCK-IT-UP-BUTTERCUP, *and abide by the law!*

The Laws:
1	I am the Creator.
8	The world is not "out there"—it is "in here."
15	To create a functional life requires one to do one's own thinking.
17	The energy to which we hold fast is what runs our life:
10	The purpose of life is for those lessons.

Questions:
- Does this remind you of any current political party?
- If so, is it about the truth—or are you just bent on ***making it so?***
- There are two sides to every argument. Have you looked for the truth in both?
- How about in the rest of your life? Do you always seek to be right?
- Or do you seek the truth?
- How about right here, right now? Are you seeking the truth?

Shit Down His Neck

As a Personal Life Coach, a potential client once questioned my honesty. Kinda took me back and I had to grin, remembering how there was a time when I would have wanted to tear his head off and shit down his neck. But I've learned a few things, like the spiritual laws—as in, *The energy out returns in kind.*

So without letting go of that grin, here is what I said: "Y'know, those who know me, know my word is good. Those who don't . . . Well, most of them can figure that out. And of the rest? . . . Most of them just view others in the light of their own paranoia"—my grin widened at the confused look on his face. I continued, "Now just where do you stand in all this?"

I paused, watching the pressure building in his psyche, then quickly gave him his opportunity to release. "Relax, lets just say that with me, you're free to chose that for yourself."

His face cleared and he shook his head a little and then began to join me with his own grin. Tapping his shoulder in a friendly way, I added. "Besides, whatever you choose, it won't change what's true—only how you feel about me."

Laws:
4   The energy out returns in kind.
8   The world is not *out there*—it is *in here.*
9   Others are but a mirror for us to see ourselves.
13   Our life is our sole possession—and so it is for everyone

Questions:
- ➤ Do you see that all he needed was for me to accept him, whether or not, he accepted me?
- ➤ Do you think the energy was loving?
- ➤ Or if not loving—do you think it was manipulative?
- ➤ Do you know that with this book, you have the right to see it however you choose? Won't change the truth—only how you see this book.

The Shit You Dwell On

Speaking of the shit your mind is dwelling on—is that truly what you want in life? Remember that Spiritual Law—

The Law:
24   What your mind dwells on with passion, is what you get.

Questions:
- Does what your mind now dwells on stink? Do you harbor unloving thoughts? Are you aware that how you see others is likely *not* how they view themselves? Can you be okay with them in knowing that they have the right to take that view—it is their life, not yours?
- Maybe you are dwelling on shit from the past. You know the past is unchangeable, don't you? Why would you want to drag that shit into your present? Don't believe in this law? Doesn't matter—it just is.
- Or maybe it's shit you are afraid will happen—shit that's only real in your mind—right now. Kinda insane to want to create that being in your present—same law. But that is what you will create—y'know?
- What is your mind dwelling on right now? *Write about it—*

Believing is Seeing

There is an old saying: "Seeing is believing." Could it be, that this thought swings both ways?—"Believing is seeing."

If you don't see it, then you don't believe it. That is about trusting only in actual fact—being *at effect* in life. But believing is a subjective term, not an actual physical property.

When you believe there is greatness in someone, then you will see it. When you believe there is greatness in you, then there will be. That is about your perceptions creating your world—about being *at cause* in life.

You are the creator of your life! And you create it all with a thought. *Everything begins as a thought*—just one of Life's Laws that you might want to remember.

Laws:
1   I am the Creator.
2   Thoughts create.
19   We Are Quintessentially, Beings of Energy:

Questions:
- Could it be that the energy of our belief in someone does actually uplift them?
- Whoa! What about their belief in you?
- What about the energy of disbelief?
- Wouldn't you rather be a source that is uplifting? It is a choice.

Anal Attracts Assholes

If your gonna be anal retentive about stuff, the only folks you can expect to attract to your cause will be assholes.

But if you're loving and accepting, you'll find yourself rubbing shoulders—not asses—with a whole different side of folks.

Laws:
3   Thoughts are energy
19 We Are Quintessentially, Beings of Energy:
4   The energy out, returns in kind.
17 The Energy To Which We Hold Fast Is What Runs Our Life
24 Whatever Our Thoughts Dwell Upon With Energy

Questions:
- Do you find yourself uplifted by those around you whose energy is loving?
- When being around those whose energy is not loving, do you feel depleted?
- If your own energy is not loving, likely you will need to be held up—validated—by others whose energy is also not loving?
- Are there people whose energy you may no longer want being in your life?
- *Write down your thoughts on it.*

Pissing on Ourselves

We all at sometime have pissed on our self. But some of us learn by it to take a moment and look first at the facts before letting fly the next time—facts like, for instance, which way the wind is blowing.

Sometimes we can't see the truth of it all because we are simply standing too close to the splatter coming off our walls. You know . . . the ones that keep our mind so narrowly enclosed.

So before you let fly, take a moment to look at the truth. Don't go against it. And if you still keep getting splattered, try opening up the walls of your mind. That may just be what your soul is trying to tell you about.

Laws:
2   Thoughts create.
15   To create a functional life requires one to do one's own thinking.
16   Controlling anything outside ourselves is a fallacy.
28   Those times when life is at its most chaotic, are the times of most opportunity.
33   Everything that happens in your life, happens for your highest good.

Questions:
   ➢ When was the last time you pissed and got splattered? Why was that, do you think?
   ➢ You *were* doing the pissing, weren't you?
   ➢ Doesn't that indicate that the problem originated with you?
   ➢ Which of these laws were you breaking?

Perfectly Fucked Up

Ah, so often it is that one hears folks complaining of how the world is so "fucked up" . . .

Yup! Truth is, they're correct: THEIR world is fucked up.

In my world, it is different. In my world if something is fucked up, it is only because of my own inability to see it all as perfection.

Yes, the world is the perfect reflection of one's own thoughts. And no one's world is ever the same.

If you don't like this "fucked up" world . . . Well then, search through your thinking. Tweak some things and find that perfection. Y'know, perfection doesn't always start out with feeling good. Hell, if you don't have a little pain and strain in your world, how are you ever going to know the ecstasy when you find it?

Laws:
8   The world is not "out there"—it is "in here."
3   Thoughts are energy.
25   Your every word is an order to your soul:

Questions:
What? I heard that thought. Let me paraphrase: *"What kinda psychobabble shit is this?"* (You sound like my ex). I'll give you an arbitrary example, and then an exercise to do.
- My world is fucked-up—no one likes me
- Tweaking my thinking: It's because I am just not likeable or attractive.
- Solution: I start noticing the things I see that are likeable and attractive about me. Each day I see more and more things and I begin taking better care of myself and my appearance.
- Pretty soon I believe it to be true that, "I AM ATTRACTIVE"—Whoa! And now others see it too. *I am suddenly very popular!*

Exercise:
➢ *Now YOU do it.*

Perfection

Your life is always perfect, just as it is. If it does not feel so, it is only because it is pointing out to you what you must change in your thinking to make it feel so. Now, *that is perfection!*

Your feelings are the guidance system keeping the missile of your life on course. And the target?—Perhaps that is something only for your soul, or what some would call the Grim Reaper to know. The point of life is not in the target, rather in the perfection of the flight—right now!

Laws:
1   I am the Creator.
8   The world is not "out there"—it is "in here."
23   All life happens right now—now is the only time there is for the living.
10   The purpose of life is for those lessons.
37   Living is a conscious choice. Consciously—but usually unconsciously—so is dying.

Questions:
- The purpose—law #10—what is the lesson or experience your soul is needing to experience right now?
- Is it something that feels "bad" or "scary?"
- Are you going to buck-up and face it, or run? Law #37 is listed for a reason. You may want to go back and read it in its entirety. *Write about that.*

Overdosing with Laxatives

Taking offense is something toxic only to yourself. It is like overdosing with laxatives with the expectation that somehow the other person is the one who will get the shits—and, you'll get even.

The act of taking offense in the first place, just goes to show others what gets your bowels in an uproar. And they see that by the fact that your choice of feelings has resulted in you shitting on yourself while blaming them for it.

Surely you don't LIKE feeling that way—and you do choose your own feelings? Well, don't you?

Laws:
1. I am the Creator.
7. Along with being the creator comes responsibility.
3. Thoughts are energy.
22. We can only feel our own feelings on a conscious level.

Questions:
- Do you actually think that just because YOU are offended, that they are required to give a shit?
- Are you aware that no matter a person's intent toward you, there can be NO offense, until you take it?
- In taking offense, you give away your power and make yourself a victim?
- Are you prepared to own that?

Do you Have OPS Disease?

If you are busy taking offense with *Other Peoples Shit*, you ain't doing anything about what's stinking about you. Fact is, you can't do a thing about the way other people's shit smells. But you can about your own.

You just need to stop talking out of your ass—as in "taking offense."

Laws:
1   I am the Creator.

Questions:
- ➢ Yeah, these last two are saying pretty-much the same thing. Did you understand at least one of them?
- ➢ Did you notice that they are examples of victim thinking—Spiritual Laws are the opposite of it, y'know?
- ➢ When you take offense with something or someone, are you not saying that you are a victim?
- ➢ Who is it that is victimizing you—really?
Hint: You only need the one law listed to give you the answer. Write about it.

Self Esteem

Those who don't give a rat's ass for what others think about them, are those who like themselves.

Conversely, those who do are those who don't.

Laws:
3   Thoughts are energy.
8   The world is not "out there"—it is "in here."
16 Controlling anything outside ourselves is a fallacy.

Questions:
- If you care about what others will think, can you ever be authentic?
- Wouldn't that demand you wear a facade that reflects who they want you to be?
- Can you truly respect others who you know aren't being real?
- Are You always being your true self, or do you bow to society's demands.

Naked in Bullshit

A fool is someone who wants to know others but is too cowardly to expose his/her true self, naked for the others to see.

Sure, that is not necessary for you to get to know them. But it is necessary if they are to know you.

Truth is, those who have the courage to show their real self, naked to you, will know when they are faced with someone clothed in their bullshit.

Do you really think they can't smell you and be repelled by your naked cowardice?

Laws:

4   The energy out, returns in kind.
9   Others are but a mirror for us to see ourselves.
14   Change is the constant of the universe.
3   Thoughts are energy.

Questions:
- Are you aware that what other people think of you is none of your business?
- Are you aware that what they see in you is only the reflection of themselves?
- The truth is, you have NO say in what others will think. People may pretend, but for most, what they think, is not what they say. Y'know?

Intimacy—In-To-Me-See

Guess maybe I look at a lot of stuff differently than most.

But just as the whole world is not with me when I'm grunting and groaning, making involuntary noises, and stinking up my bathroom, they are also not privy to what some might consider my more odious thoughts. *But in reading this, you are.*

Few would deny that this book stinks. Do you think I'm offering you a peek at my bottom line? Do you feel privileged to be privy to my privy?

My greatest wish is that you understand that a smell is just a smell. *It's your judgments that say it stinks*. Maybe that is the one understanding—the one precious jewel to take away from this book.

And maybe when someone you meet in life gets real personal and honest with you, you won't feel repelled like most folks do.

Maybe you will have the courage to do the same in return.

--- — — — ---

Laws:
4   The energy out, returns in kind.
9   Others are but a mirror for us to see ourselves.

Questions:
- ➢ Oh . . . my . . . God! I just repeated myself again. Which one did you hear?
- ➢ Didn't hear it? Okay, I'll do it again—soon . . .

Should-ing

"Should" is just the shit from between someone's ears—remember? If you insist on "should-ing" on yourself or others, ya gotta know that you'll always be the one who comes out stinking.

When on yourself, it is saying that what you think is not what you do—you are out of integrity.

And when should-ing on others—the stink of you is dropping down from your perch above, like a pigeon, roosting in the eaves above their door.

Laws:
11   Self-esteem requires integrity—it is the respect of your soul.
13   Our life is our sole possession—and so it is for everyone.

Questions:
- When was the last time you *should* on yourself?
- Why didn't you do what you said you *should* have done?
- Do you *should* on yourself more often than you *should* on others?
- Given the above, what is that saying about you? *Write about it.*

I Am the Creator . . . Remember?

I don't get to blame others for anything created in my life. This is one of those rules to live by—one of Life's Laws.

Yet, there is something to be said about the energy—mine, and of others. I choose the energy in which I live . . . and of those with whom I associate.

We are social creatures. Just as we need food to sustain our bodies, we need loving energy to sustain our souls.

Bad food or bad energy . . . The surest way to get diarrhea is to shit where you eat, or feed where someone else shits.

It's real simple: don't hang around with people who're talking shit! If you do, you'll find your own mouth spewing it too—*you've done caught diarrhea!* Like energies attract.

Laws:
3	Thoughts are energy.
4	The energy out, returns in kind.
9	Others are but a mirror for us to see ourselves.
17	The energy to which we hold fast is what runs our life:

Questions:
- ➢ When was the last time you were hanging around with someone and realized how bad their energy was?
- ➢ Did you find yourself also putting out a like energy?
- ➢ Ever thought about stepping up onto the curb, out of that gutter?

About the Sorriest Ass

Someone offers you something that you really need, so you accept. Then you learn that it was something that they needed for them self—for their own sustenance in life. Are they truly this wonderful, caring, generous, person that everyone seems to be saying they are?

Or are they just another sorry-assed martyr? One saying—as all martyrs do—"I'm better than you, because I'm suffering. And, it's all because of you!" Then they whine about being crucified by those very people who they are "suffering" for. That part is true.

Duh!

Martyrs . . . Yeah, you got it. Wish there was, but there is not much positive to be said about them. Don't you wonder how it is that so many in the world have no clue?—Or do they? Those who are about negativity and hatred sure seem to have found a very useful purpose for martyrs. Strap them with explosives and send them out to blow up a few hundred innocents. Useful for them, but not very loving for the rest of us.

And still . . . Perhaps it is the martyrs of this world who will teach this planet the truth about love—by showing us all, the essence of what it is not.

Sure, martyrs often are seen to crawl up on their crosses all by themselves. That is not the whole of it. Yes, the martyr gives his/her life's blood to the struggle. But there is that other half of martyrdom—the half that glamorizes the drama. It's a vicious, cycle—a circle—a rolling engine of control and drama, that takes only the loss of one of its halves to flatten and stop.

Martyrs . . . Truly, when the whole world sees them as the sorriest asses on the planet, the cycle of misery will stop. And maybe—just maybe—the love can begin.

--- — — ---

Laws:
21   Real love, once given, cannot be taken back. Unless you have love within you, for yourself, you have none to give another.

Questions:
- ➤ Do you admire someone who would *give you their only shirt off their back?*
- ➤ Would you think less of them if they had another for themselves?
- ➤ How about if they had more for others?
- ➤ Can you understand why this last question strikes at the truth of what's admirable?

Washing Off the Bullshit

Remember the fish out of water—how he doesn't even know water until he's out of it?—How it is that by being in the air, in being immersed in something different, he comes to know about water?

In our world it's like someone who steps out and washes off all their bullshit. They never saw the facade of it before it was gone. And it usually takes a great calamity—a storm—in one's life to wash it away.

But once seeing it gone—and how much better life smells—why would they ever want to step back into it. Once out, one can recognize others who are like themselves, but the rest of the world just sees such a person as a little "out of it."

Ah, but let's take it back to you, the fish. Don't you yearn to be one of the few fish who no longer swims in that cess-pool?

------ - - - - ------

Laws:
8   The world is not "out there"—it is "in here."
10   The purpose of life is for those lessons.

Questions:
- Can you see it—smell it? Are you wanting to jump out of the cess pool?
- Or are you too afraid? Don't fish that jump out of the fish bowl generally die? What's outside your pool is the unknown.
- Are you just comfortable hanging onto the other turds floating in your cesspool, just hoping you won't drown?
- And yup—Did you catch that I'm talking about that façade, once again? Being real is so different from being like the others. The cost—you'll have to swim in your own pool. The reward—some really good people will want to swim with you. Do you see it?

Constipation

Whether it's what you ate, or the feelings you hold onto in life, such things need nurture, provide growth to one's body or spirit, then pass on through. Shit's shit! And constipation is just not healthy.

Laws:
6   The energy of thoughts must flow:
17   The energy to which we hold fast is what runs our life:
24   Whatever our thoughts dwell upon with energy is what we are attracting into our life right now.

Questions:
- Is there something that someone once did to you that you just can't forgive?
- How about something that happened that you can't accept?
- What if you took responsibility, went over the above questions and changed the word *can't* to *won't?* It is all a choice, y'know?
- Do you know that when you don't accept "what is," you guarantee yourself pain?
- Do you see that when that pain is about "what was," it guarantees your life will SUCK painfully—now?
- Do you know that the past is unchangeable? Every time you make "what was" unacceptable, you drag that past into your present—and you still can't change it.
- *Write about how this affects your life.*

Explosive Diarrhea

Ever feel like your life is like a case of explosive diarrhea? Those are the best times because you get to flush the old crap out and bring in something new.

'Course, you gotta know that it's not something "out there?" It's something in you—in your mind—that has contaminated it all. That is what has put your life in the crapper.

Yeah, when you get right down to it. You're gonna find that it always revolves around the way you think about something. And *that,* you can change—once you see what is so stinkin' about your thinkin'.

Good thing about it all?—You can change your thinking just as easily as you can change that pair of shitty shorts.

Change your mind—change your life. It really is that simple!

---- — — — ----

Laws:
8   The world is not "out there"—it is "in here."
28   Those times when life is at its most chaotic, are the times of most opportunity.

Questions:
- So what is it right now, that has your bowels in an uproar?
- What is it that serves you to feel that way?
- How could you view it that would serve you as well, or better—without the gastric fireworks?

Rude and Crude

Rude and *Crude* . . . Yes, I've been called both. Crude is a descriptive term saying that I am basic: not sophisticated, unpolished. I choose to accept it as being likened to "an uncut" diamond—a compliment to who I am, being basic to all that I might become.

Rude is a different matter. . . . A term of judgment, it speaks not of who I am, but of who you are–your judgments in how you view me in your world. Like all thoughts spoken from your ass, it's a matter of embarrassment— not for me, but for you. And too, only those who think the same would be immune to the odor.

--- --- --- --- ---

Laws:
5   The Universe always balances.
8   The world is not "out there"—it is "in here."

Questions:
> ➢ Most books dealing with Spiritual Law are written on an esoteric cloud—somewhere *up there,* floating around feeling good. Do you want to feel good—or do you want change in your life?
> ➢ You are aware that change is scary and never feels good until it is done and becomes the norm?
> ➢ Are you someone who would never smell the stink if someone didn't rub your shit into your face?
> ➢ If you are—and you're still reading—then welcome to the redneck side of town. *Write about it.*

Slinging Shit

Pissing on someone else's parade is one thing . . . but slinging shit? When you're slinging shit at other people, you need to remember that everyone then gets to see the deepest darkest slimiest most repugnant stuff, inside of you.

Sure, everyone understands that you felt pressured by your own internal sense of right and wrong and responded that way.

There is an expression: *When you squeeze oranges, orange juice comes out. Why?—Because that's what is in them!*

It doesn't help anyone, just knowing that it is *not* about them. Rather, it's about your own personal sense of right and wrong that squeezes you into targeting them. And too, they know that the screaming yellow squirts coming at them, is not orange juice.

Can anyone ever feel safe around you?

——— — — — ———

Laws:
1   I am the Creator.
3   Thoughts are energy.
7   Along with being the creator comes responsibility.

Questions:
- Can you see that the core issue here revolves around the energy of your thinking—love or fear?
- And about responsibility (Law #1)?
- And about blame?(Law #7)
- *Write down your thoughts.*

Shame-ings & Should-ings

There are many things that obstruct our ability to know and give love; shame is only one.

"Shame-ings" and "should-ings"—such are as the feces of other people's minds, that they would heap upon us.

To accept it does not mean we will be fertilized and grow; it just means our viewpoint of life will be obstructed and stink.

Laws:
15 To create a functional life requires one to do one's own thinking.
2 Thoughts create.
7 Along with being the creator comes responsibility.

Questions:
- How do you feel about someone rubbing all that should on you?
- How about when they try to lay shame by telling you how badly your life stinks?
- Do you have a better grasp on what those words mean?
- Do you see how they are meant to control your life?
- Will they—in the future? *Write about it.*

Falling Out of Integrity

Say what you think—then don't put the lie to it by what you do.

And if you slip on that one, then have the cajones to admit it. Lift your ride back upright. Pick the gravel outta your ass—clean up any mess (might have to change your shorts). Then kick her over and get on with the ride.

Yep! Kinda hurts to fall out of integrity . . . dontcha think?

Laws:

11 Self-esteem requires integrity—it is the respect of your soul.
28 Those times when life is at its most chaotic, are the times of most opportunity.

Questions:
- Everyone's integrity slips once in a while? When was the last time yours did?
- Did you clean up your mess with others involved and climb back on?
- How about with yourself?
- Or are you still laying on the blacktop bleeding and expecting someone will come along and save you from facing it?

Pull it Out

Even I don't like to admit that when my nose gets to pointing way up high—means that the stick that props it up needs to be removed from my ass once again.

Yeah, I know. Maybe that sounds a little pessimistic. But optimistic—pessimistic . . . this book can be taken either way.

Point is: To make your future be any better, you've got to first see the truth about you—right now.

Laws:
23   All life happens right now—now is the only time there is for the living:
2   Thoughts create.
4   The energy out, returns in kind.
8   The world is not "out there"—it is "in here."
10   The purpose of life is for those lessons.

Questions:
- Remember me saying "This is not a feely-good workbook?" Is this one of those not-so-good times?
- Is there something stinking up your life that your ego doesn't want to look at?
- Will you look?
- "No, there isn't," you say? It's okay, come back later when you're willing. There isn't a person alive who doesn't fart once in a while—

Not "Normal"

The truth about life is that—whether we are willing to admit it or not—we all have a need to be *loved* by the others around us.

But wait! Wouldn't that require you to be some kind of Saint?

So okay . . . Most of us would settle for just being *liked.*

Still too tall an order? How about *respected*? Or even *feared*?

So what's this saying about the world? Could it be that what is *normal* in this world is that when we don't get the love we need from others, we lie just a little to ourselves and lower the bar of what we think we deserve? Easier than holding ourselves capable of *being* more loving, and therefore *deserving* more love.

Easier still is to simply put on the face of who we think others will love/like/respect/or fear. Lets face it: what's *normal* in this world is to wear a facade. Hopefully—for our acceptance of them—the others will at least pretend they believe it is real (their facade).

So lets look at what else it means to be *normal* in this world.

Isn't it just *all-too-normal* to slam-dunk those we don't like, and to get ours—win—whether someone else has to lose or not? Well . . . isn't it? Isn't that the basic concept behind most all athletics? Don't we make heroes out of those who do just that?

It is *normal* to return violence with violence even though, on some level, we all know the law of spirit is that the energy out is the energy that will return—sure as gravity.

The *normal* way in this world is to destroy what we think is unacceptable, instead of building something that is.

It is *normal* to tell others only what we don't like, rather than to put forth, up front, what we do. To tell them what we won't accept instead of just accepting.

It is *normal* to try to control those around us—to make them *be* who *we* want them *to be.*

Yes, it is *normal* to set people up to lose with us instead of to win—to tell them nothing at all up front—to find it more enjoyable seeing them drown rather than to teach them, and see them swim.

There's no denying it: The truth about me is that I am *not normal.* I don't want to be! But it would be nice to be with others of like mind.

The simple truth of it is, shit flows downhill. That's *normal.* But don't we who see that flow owe it to ourselves to buck the flow of what's *normal*—maybe even to climb out before we slide into the cesspool and drown.

——— — — — ———

Laws:
Which law to list? This one seems to cover them all, but to choose one
15   To create a functional life requires one to do one's own thinking.

Questions:
- Can you agree that what is considered *normal* in this world—STINKS?
- Wouldn't you rather be *not normal*—like me?
- *Write about it.*

Getting Real

"Getting real" is not about telling others what you think about them, rather what you know about you. It is not about saying what they should be ashamed of, rather what you are ashamed of.

It is not about calling them a coward, rather admitting to the fears you haven't yet stepped through. *Getting real is not about them, rather about you—get it?*

Yup. Most think it takes courage. To actually—be real—to face your fears about what others think.

What if that were just one of society's lies? The one that demands having a facade—a pretense—of what others want you to be, in order to be acceptable? That is what societies rules are all designed to make you be—a fake—a phony—a coward. . . .

Truth is: it is not about courage. It is just about letting go of what others think of you. Yes, you WILL pay societies price by being unacceptable with some.

And, you WILL then know who doesn't belong in your life—and who does. A fair exchange don't you think?

Laws:
9   Others are but a mirror for us to see ourselves.
17   The energy to which we hold fast is what runs our life:
26   Change requires truth.

Questions:
- To point out someone else's faults in order to smoke-screen your own—isn't that akin to blame?
- You being real—and not giving a shit about what others think—can you see how that erases all that foolish fear?
- Can you see that it doesn't have to take courage—or smoke-screens to be real? It just takes a big "FUCK YOU" to society.
- Are you willing?
- You cannot be REAL while wearing society's facade. Do you see that? *Write about it.*

The MO Game

My parents haven't accepted me since I divorced my wife. The following is an excerpt from my side of a conversation I had with a very beautiful woman who wanted to intercede and go talk to my parents (who by-the-way are of the Mormon faith and philosophy).

***

You, visit my folks? No. Don't want to play the Mo game. You know, the one where you gotta be—or rather, PRETEND to be—who they want, or you're just not okay.

***

Played that game most of my life—not playing anymore—that's why I stopped visiting them. Y'know? Sadly, it is the only way not to play the game.

***

For you to go would be upping the ante. That is, you'd be asking them to be different—to pretend to be someone who accepts me. Just a picture of the same game taken from another angle.

***

The truth about what it means to accept someone is simply that you don't try to change them. I accept them. And accepting someone being who they want to be doesn't mean that you want to be around them

***

Yes, I wish it were not so. I wish I could just be there and love them without all the drama—drama of them trying to change me—drama of having my love for them held hostage in the name of control. It is always painful when that drama is in my face telling me once again that I am not acceptable unless I'm living my life their way. And so I stay away....

* * *

Seriously—you see me as too intense? And judgmental?

* * *

I heave a deep breath watching her back as she walks away. Yes, my thought system serves me well in keeping those ladies away who can't understand, and won't accept me.

She doesn't understand that it is the same game, that she offers to play. The prize is love. But it cannot be won playing—only by not playing. She couldn't—no wouldn't—accept the love that I have offered her.

Laws:
8   The world is not "out there"—it is "in here."
13 Our life is our sole possession—and so it is for everyone.
17 The energy to which we hold fast is what runs our life:
5   The Universe always balances.

Questions:
- When was the last time you tried to change someone's perception of you?
- How'd that work out? It didn't? That's to be expected.
- Oh, it did? Wow! Are you *that* good at pretense—or is that a hook I see stuck in your cheek?

Hung-Up

Chuck didn't *get it*. Perhaps he never will . . .

"Chuck, what do you mean 'morality?' Morality has nothing to do with integrity." I watched his face screw in determined agitation at my words.

"It sure does! How can you be in integrity without having morality?"

"Chuck, morality is one of those personal judgment calls that we all seem to get so hung-up over."

"Hung-up over?"

"Yeah . . . You know: Nobody's morality is ever the same. Kinda like 'right' and 'wrong,' you decide it for yourself in your own mind."

"Right' and 'wrong?'"—Chuck's nose was beginning to redden— "What the hell do you mean about right and wrong. The bible says—"

"The Bible? C'mon Chuck! Now you're beginning to sound like one of the "moral majority." Don't let what someone told you the Bible means get you all hung-up. Do your own thinkin'."

"There you go with that 'hung-up' stuff again!"—there was no dissuading Chuck from his crusade—"I want to know just what you consider 'integrity' means—and how you can have it without morality!"

Well, to me, integrity means that what is in my heart, what I'm saying, and what I'm doing, is all the same thing. Unlike morality, integrity is about matching my thoughts with what actually 'is.' It's kinda like the fabric of my personal power—that is, it holds my life together, on track first with myself, and then with others. It doesn't require I meet anyone's moral standards but my own."

"Well, people can't just do what they want—others be-damned—not and have integrity!"

" Chuck, you might not like them, but if they're doing what they want and what they say, you always know what they stand for—that's integrity."

"But morality . . ."

"Ah, Chuck there you go again, getting yourself all hung-up." The vein in his forehead now threatened to explode. "Look, Chuck . . . Let me take it all down to its most basic terms. "You see . . . 'Hung-up' does describe it all perfectly. Have you ever seen two dogs fuck?"

"What?"

"Yeah, you know . . . How they get hung-up together at the end?" Chuck's mouth was open now, but nothing seemed forthcoming. I continued. "Do you know why that is?"

Silence—

"It's because that's the way they're built. Swells up in the middle so's they don't have to think about it. Time they get loose, the one's pregnant."

"What the hell does that have to do with anything?"

"Well, its just that our species doesn't have that excuse. If we get hung-up while screwing around with one another—physically or otherwise—it's because we have a knot in the middle of our thinking. That knot is called 'morality.'"

"You're not making any sense!"

"Look . . . Chuck, consider this: What if we took all that morality—and all that right and wrong that it's comprised of—and just shit-canned it all?" I grinned at him now. *Damn but he was fun to talk with!* "What if then, whenever we get tempted to root around in the garbage for some brainless rule to tell us how to behave, we instead just replace it all with this question: 'Is this loving?'"

From the look now on his face, I knew where I stood with Chuck. I sighed. Yeah, it was fun to talk with him. But now he wasn't talking, and I had to ask myself the question: *Is this now loving? Does it feel good not only outwardly, but also in my heart?* I shut-up. In the silence there were suddenly answers. Funny, how they arrived as questions: *Was I so unloving that so many, like Chuck, were so unloving of me? Was being and thinking the same as they, the only Vaseline that would get me over their lumps? Indeed, did I have one of my own?—Whoa! Could it be that two hard-headed old male dogs would simply get along much better if they didn't fuck with one another?*

PART THREE
Relationships

I Am the Creator

That is the law—inescapable.

My Universe—all of it—is self-created. It exists foremost and ultimately, only in my mind. My mind chooses how I will view everything, and my view is my reality about everything . . . and especially, about everyone.

Are they good, or evil? Considerate, or selfish? Fair, or conniving? Beautiful, or ugly? I decide the correct labels to paste onto everyone I know. And I choose whether to like them—or even, to love them.

But sometimes the things that person does, tends to clash with my label. For those I care little for, it is no problem to correct the label. After all, everyone knows that the truth of who someone is, can be found, not in the 'who' they say they are, but the 'who' they are being. Right?

Still, for those we choose to love? It is so easy to ignore the things they do that don't fit our labels. Somehow their labels just don't seem to come off so easily. Somehow the ink on them is more indelible. Hell, it's even possible that a man can love a woman for twenty-five years and never see that who she is, in her world—and in the worlds of others—is not the same person he knows. How many men go to their graves loving a woman who only exists as a lie in their own mind?

Ah, but sometimes the Specter of Death can be so loving—so nourishing—as to pause at a man's death bed and whisper the ultimatum:

"Your soul will no longer tolerate living the lies.
If you want to go on living, it must be done in truth!"

Yes, for me it was exactly so. When next I looked upon the wife I loved, the label that said "Her Love" suddenly looked different. What did it now say under the light of her actions?—"Her need." But need of what?

Oh, my God! Of course! Why didn't I ever see it before? *Security!* **I was her security.**

But wait! There was that that other Spiritual Law:

"Change your mind: change your life."

Somehow my world had shifted! Changed! And change never feels secure. So, who was I then to her?

Ah . . . Of course. I was changed. I no longer acted and reacted the same: In her world, it seemed her label on me now said *"CRAZY!"*

The only real question I needed ask, was: "Who is this woman now to me?" My mind wanted to say: "She is my lover, my loyal friend, my soul mate!—the beautiful woman I possess, but don't deserve."

But my heart knew different . . .

There was that label I'd placed upon myself: "Undeserving!" Somehow now, it had lost it's prefix—for me, at least.

Then who was she now?—this illusion that once was? Was she still beautiful to me in the light of truth? Oh yes! Most certainly so—on the outside.

Ah well—*sigh*. Doesn't much matter now. Perhaps she was right. Perhaps, I am crazy.

Certainly it is so in her world—wherever that is now.

FLUSH!

--- — — — ---

Laws:
1   I am the Creator.
8   The world is not "out there"—it is "in here."
14   Change is the constant of the universe.
28   Those times when life is at its most chaotic, are the times of most opportunity.

Questions:
- Are there any lies you are refusing to look at in your own life?
- What would the price be—how would your life change—if you looked?
- Would you rather pay that price, than to wait for your soul to hit the reset button?
- Is my own story here, possibly the last warning your soul may give?
- No, of course not—but *wait!* Is that even possible do you think?

>>><<<

Perfect Love

In the imperfection of our expectations some say: There are no perfect people. That's not true—EVERY one of us is perfect. But as to perfect LOVE—that's different.

The trick is in just finding people who are being who they truly are, then in loving them without trying to change them. Now *that* is perfect love.

Laws:
13   Our life is our sole possession—and so it is for everyone.
21   Real love, once given, cannot be taken back.

Questions:
- In looking at someone as a possible mate, have you ever heard someone say "They've got potential?"
- Does that say they accept that possible mate exactly as they are now?
- Is there any such thing as "perfect potential?"
- Have you ever found yourself taking part in the shit-storm that follows when one person tries to change another? Write—

Wanted: One Honest Woman

A woman who wants her man, just as he is; not as her make-over would have him pretending to be.

(Accepts him)

A woman who would choose to be happy with her man; rather than expecting him to make her happy.

(Takes responsibility for her choice of feelings)

A woman who would rather her man commit to valuing a relationship he is free to leave; rather than committing to a relationship that has no such freedom.

(Understands the underlying lie concerning marriage)

A woman who makes her relationship a safe place to be, even at those times when she is most unhappy with it.

(Doesn't require him to pay the price of her feelings)

A woman who will say "Tomorrow is my birthday and here is what I want;" rather than, "My birthday was yesterday—ASSHOLE!"

(Sets him up to win with her).

A woman who admires her man's cajones all the time; not just when his dick is standing up out of the way.

(Respects men)

A woman who likes riding her man's fast motorcycle, soft tongue, and hard dick, all equally well— Well okay, so make that, her "machismo" man's. . . ."

(Is honest about sex, uninhibited, and unafraid).

——— — — ———

Laws:
7   Along with being the creator comes responsibility.

Exercise:
- ➤ The reason Law #7 is the only one listed is because it concerns the questions of responsibility, façade, and of blame. If you are responsible for how they see, and feel about you—blame—then you must wear a façade to be acceptable. Correct?
- ➤ But if you see them as responsible for how you see and feel—blame—then they need to wear a façade of their own. Correct?
- ➤ It is the bottom-line reason people are not honest with one another. Kinda sucks, doesn't it? *Write about it.*

Shit Comes of Being Nourished

Back to that central theme of this book: there is one surety of life that we don't usually like to acknowledge: *We all shit!*

Those who are wise will appreciate the kernel of food—or the grain of truth—that has been brought into and nourished our lives . . . and then flush it! But others aren't appreciative and of course, never see the need to flush.

They most often choose not to be nourished. They refuse to hear the message and the change it would inspire, but instead carry their mental shit around with them. And it always smells bad—at least to others.

They're used to it. Though it may be painfully heavy—though it may bend their lives grotesquely, even be crippling, most fear the pain of what they would see, were they to truly look.

Oh sure, most everyone knows that fear is an illusion. In this case, keeping us from accepting the nourishment—and then from flushing. But the pain we sometimes feel at letting go of our illusions can be real. It is mental pain—sure. Pain we do to ourselves—yes. But it is real, very real! It is only that fearful pain that needs flushing.

——— — — — ———

Laws:
2   Thoughts create.
3   Thoughts are energy.
6   The energy of thoughts must flow:
8   The world is not "out there"—it is "in here."

Questions:
- ➢ Society demands that we all put on a pretense—a façade. Can you see how dysfunctional it is not to be real?
- ➢ Can anyone ever know you and love you if you don't let them see the real you?
- ➢ Why is it when you are laying your true self bare—naked for others to see—you so often are ostracized?
- ➢ Could that be because those others recognize your truth, and your courage, and are unwilling to match it? *Write about it.*

Shit in an Ice Cream Cone

What is it about prejudging people—about being aware, of noticing what they say, their words and, their body language, and of what they do, or don't do? Is it about their integrity—or something more?

Then, when something's not showing up as true . . . Well, you know what to do.

If it looks like shit and smells like shit, it doesn't matter if it comes in an ice cream cone. Do you really need to taste it?

No matter how pretty the package, some people are best left untasted in life.

Laws:
11   Self-esteem requires integrity—it is the respect of your soul.
3   Thoughts are energy.
32   There is no good or bad, right or wrong, it is all God.

Questions:
- Does this thought seem judgmental?
- You're correct, it is. Did you read the entirety of Law #32?
- Do you agree? *Write about that.*

Hi Ho Silver. . . .

What is it about the hero always riding off into the sunset? I used to believe he was being a martyr—giving up the woman in self-sacrifice because he could not love her well.

Perhaps it was really because he needed the time alone to heal his pain from the one who couldn't, or rather wouldn't, love him well.

Either way, was he really a hero? Did he have the courage to take responsibility for, and to face his feelings? And martyr?—Holy shit! Good thing he rode off before someone hung him from a tree—or a cross.

Laws:
3   Thoughts are energy.
4   The energy out, returns in kind.
7   Along with being the creator comes responsibility.
21   Real love, once given, cannot be taken back:

Questions:
➢ Do you ever "ride off into the sunset" rather than stay and face, and accept, what is?
➢ Did you ever love someone who wouldn't return your love?
➢ Did/do you hate them for it?

Exercise:
➢ *Either way, read Law # 21 in its entirety and re-consider.*

The Game of Control

Playing the game of control with a woman is something a man can't win. Give it over to her, and she'll carry your balls in her pocket forever.

Try to take control of her and you're sure to wind up with your dick in your zip. Then, guess who you'll go whimpering to for help in getting it out?

Unlike sex, control is only satisfying when you play it with yourself. Play the game of sex with your lady. Control is for when your playing it solitaire.

But finding a woman who won't insist on playing the game of control with you—now, that's a real slippery thing to find.

Laws:

13   Our life is our sole possession—and so it is for everyone.
16   Controlling anything outside ourselves is a fallacy.
4   The energy out, returns in kind.

Questions:
- Is your thought system such that you need to control those around you?
- Makes for a lot of drama, doesn't it?
- Isn't it really just your feelings you are trying to control through them?
- But wait—if you were to take responsibility for your own feelings, would you ever need to control them?
- Do you think your life might then have a lot less drama?
- If you are both busy controlling the other is that out of love or fear?
- Where is there any room for love in your relationship?

I've Touched Them

It ain't them that likes me. It ain't them that hates me. . . .

I've touched them all. The first in validation and/or acceptance; the rest in opportunity—the opportunity of recognizing something within themselves that they may see, because of the mirror of me. That is assuming they know the Spiritual Law.

It's really them that don't give a shit who worry me. Either I'm so far ahead that *they* don't connect, or so far behind, that *I* don't connect.

You know, we all just have a need to touch others; be understood, and accepted. Only those who know, and apply the law, can accept the lessons in the meaning of another's unwelcome touch.

In other words: When they fart, instead of taking offense, we recognize the smell of our own shit.

Laws:
9   Others are but a mirror for us to see ourselves.
7   Along with being the creator comes responsibility.

Questions:
- When someone does something we don't like, are they responsible for our feelings?
- That is what we have all been taught—to ***blame*** others for our own choice of feelings. Do you see the lie?
- Do you see how that lie blinds us from even seeing the mirror?
- Will you be looking in the mirror?

Picking Scabs

Freshly single women? Yikes! For most, the wounds are still bleeding?

It's just that those who haven't healed, usually just hook up with guys who are also wounded, and just want to pick one another's scabs. They're not ready for someone who will help heal the wounds.

Me? I've healed. And I've helped heal—a time or two. Not really into all that anymore, y'know?

No. I'm just wanting a woman who's already healed and is looking for a Spiritual Warrior with a lot of scars?

Laws:
- 10   The purpose of life is for those lessons.
- 18   Soul to soul pacts are made in the pre-existence.
- 17   The energy to which we hold fast is what runs our life.
- 5   The Universe always balances.

Questions:
- ➢ Do you seek our others, also hurting, for mutual support?
- ➢ Or do you seek out someone who has been wounded—and has healed— and seek support?
- ➢ To feed on the energy of one—or be uplifted by the energy of the other?
- ➢ Duh! Isn't it a no-brainer? *Write about it.*

A Taste of Honey

A taste of honey here—and there,—and everywhere possible . . .

Yeah, I can understand why that's the way of it for so many guys. But in the end those guy can't help but wind up with a sticky face and nothing else . . . y'know?

Me? I prefer to just love the one I'm with—and be honest about it. Sure, so far that's meant that one of us always chooses to move on. But sticky or not, what's on my face when she turns to leave, has never been stinky.

Someday we'll both be who the other wants . . . And just "stick."Meanwhile every woman I meet gives me a gift and returns my honesty.

――――― ― ― ― ―――――

Laws:
3   Thoughts are energy.
8   The world is not "out there"—it is "in here."
10   The purpose of life is for those lessons.
34   The heart wants what the heart wants.

Questions:
- Do you believe relationships are about commitment?
- Isn't that about being there even when you don't want to be?
- What about them? Would you want someone to be/stay with you if they didn't want to?
- Do you think maybe that is a lie our society has taught us to believe?
- Perhaps we have accepted that lie because we don't have the courage to keep putting ourselves out and learning the lessons of each new person? *Write about it?*

>>><<<

A Fart in the Car

Let's face it: farting in the car is something that when alone, we all savor—ooh-yeah, good one! But when we are not alone. Then is when we open the window, and blame it on the dog—"Damn dog! Whatcha been feeding him anyway?"

And sure, blaming it on the dog is not really being honest—I mean, if I can savor my own farts, why couldn't I savor yours as well? If I felt as close to you as I do me, could I then? Maybe this is the kind of closeness we both could strive for—maybe then, if one farted, the other would just say. "Ooh-yeah! Good one Babe!"

But would I *ever,* savor that dog's farts? Nah! Don't think so. If the dog farts in the car, I'll damn sure open the window! And, I'll fervently hope that the spot—the one on the upholstery—is not some juicy little tidbit he left behind.

Bottom-line: We accept the smell of what comes out of our ass, simply because we have to—I mean—we kinda need to accept ourselves. So maybe, ladies, when next your husband farts in the car? Consider saying. "Ooh-yeah! Good one Honey."

Ya gotta know that he's likely just testing the air of your acceptance . . . dontcha think?

———   — — —   ———

Laws:
3   Thoughts are energy.
4   The energy out, returns in kind.
8   The world is not "out there"—it is "in here."

Questions:
- Could you love someone with that intensity?
- How about accepting them just so?
- Want to give it a try?
- Do you accept him to the extent that you would accept the essence of his sex—his semen—and just swallow?
- Isn't it just a simple choice of mind, how you think about him/her? *Write about it.*

Monogamy By Choice

Monogamy by choice is awesome: Monogamy by demand, just stinks.

To place any restrictions upon a relationship means your love is conditional. Should your love be unconditional, and each has the freedom to do anything they want, that does not mean they will want sex with anyone besides yourself. Nor does it mean that it would have to be a problem if they did.

Conditions mean control, and control is the major cock-block to real love. Real love simply does not exist in the same space as control. Monogamy by mutual choice is fine, but it needs to be backed by honesty above all else. Real love cannot exist without honesty. And honesty in the space of love means each has the right to be who they are without penalty. For that to be so, monogamy by choice is then as a fart in the wind.

Yet two people in love—real love—means that no matter what happens, that love will survive and they will remain together so long as both want it to be so. Should they part, the love will still survive in the heart who's love was true—one or both.

Laws:
7   Along with being the creator comes responsibility.
8   The world is not "out there"—it is "in here."

Questions
- There needs always be honest communication without consequences, between couples for the relationship to be functional—or loving. Do you agree? *Write—*
- There is "making love, and there is "fucking." Agreed? *Write—*
- Some couples can do both within the relationship. Others want more variety in their "fucking." You are either compatible in that, or not—if not, move on to someone who is. Do you see that?
- Again, "honesty and communication." When one is not free to be honest, that is when the cheating begins—it's NOT a SEXUAL issue, it IS an HONESTY issue. Real love cannot exist without honesty. Do you agree? *Write—*

Getting It Off Your Chest

"Getting it off your chest" is about releasing the pressure. About dealing with the twists and turns in your relationship.

But you've got to realize: it will likely go off like a wet fart. The shit will be real: it's *your* shit! And, it's in *your* pants.

You might first ask yourself if you really need to do that in front of your partner—or, if it would be better to deal with it yourself, by yourself.

If you don't like the consequences, you've got to remember: they may have cooked it for you, but you are the one who chose to eat the chile.

You play your part in the relationship. So don't blame them if it is burning your ass

Laws:
1   I am the Creator.
7   Along with being the creator comes responsibility.
13   Our life is our sole possession—and so it is for everyone.

Questions:
- Is this one of those small shit issues that you are building into a big turd?
- Considering Law #1, what was your part in the creating of *your* problem here?
- Is the problem about something someone did—or didn't—do?
- What do you need to change about *your* thinking to be at peace with it?
- If it was about something you did—or didn't do—what can you do to make it a win/win?

Real Men & Cretins

"So how? . . . Coach Egorhh," a woman once asked. "How can you say it's not about them. That it is of my own creation. This . . . this unfeeling cretin, being in my life?"

I thought about it and then shared with her of my own experience of women. But I told it as a story about how a young child once ran to his mommy crying over a skinned knee. And of her answer to him: "Shhhhh . . . you don't want people to think you're a baby—now do you? Real men don't cry!"

And later other tears—tears when the neighborhood bully had blackened the child's eye. "Hush! Don't shame me!" She'd answered. "Fight your own fights, and don't let that bully see you cry!"

And of when he'd crashed and twisted the bars on his new bike.— "Don't worry, when he gets home from work, your father will fix that bike. That's what men are for."

And then there were the tears over the loss of his pet . . . Over poor Lobo out there smashed into the roadway. "Get the shovel, Son," his father said. "He was just a smelly old dog. Nothing to bother your mother about—you know how she is . . . Buck-up for your mother, Boy! Go and bury the mess. Maybe later we'll get you another dog."

And about much later—I told her about when his marriage had ended. How when he began to go out with other women: Women who didn't want to hear about it. Women who dumped him one after another, because of his pain—because he tried to express it.

"Why are you telling me about some sissy little mamma's boy? No woman wants a man to cry on her shoulder." My client replied. "A shoulder to cry on—That's what they're supposed to provide for us. But instead, all they seem to want is to screw us."

Mamma's boys?—Cretin? I sighed, then tried another track "Isn't fixing things part of his job title as a 'Man.' Perhaps in his little cretin mind, when a woman shares her pain over a failed relationship, it is okay for her to be the 'sissy.' The thought in his mind then goes more like this:

> *Yikes! I know she doesn't want to hear about how I too, know such pain. Besides, she's right! The guy was an unfeeling dweeb. Yeah, I hear you, Babe. A slob!—A no-good, rotten, son-of-a-bitch . . . a cretin! But give me a chance, I've got just the tool to fix things—and I want to fix things for you. I know what I needed back then; when I was in your place; when I didn't feel I'd ever be loved again. You just need to be loved by a real man."*

"But I don't care how men think. That's got nothing to do with me!" Continued the woman. "Well . . . Does it?"

Knowing how you can't provide ears for another's deaf mind, I sighed. "I don't know," I bottom-lined it. "Perhaps you too, subconsciously bought the same messages. Perhaps your definition of a real mans is the same as that of an unfeeling cretin. Let's see: big and tough and silent—never shares his pain—only real use is to make money, and fix things. Oh and yes—even comes with his own built-in screw driver."

She looked at me in total confusion, and I continued. "Why is a man a *cretin* when he is just following the lessons you taught him? And a *sissy-boy* if he tries to learn and evolve because of them?"

Laws:
7 Along with being the creator, comes responsibility.
8 The world is not "out there"—it is "in here."

Questions:
- ➢ This one illustrates some of the lies we have been taught to believe—the worst of which, is "blame." Do you see that—or am I just another "cretin?" *Write—*

>>><<<

Soul Mates

Soul Mates? Some say there ain't no such thing. I agree—unless of course you are talking about that perfect person who comes into your life and rubs all your own shit into your face for you to look at.

Ah, but cheer-up! That shit starts to smell much better when your mind has risen spiritually above the height of your anus—and it can't do that unless it has seen the truth about your shit.

So, well . . . Maybe there is such a thing as a "soul mate." It must take someone who is loving on a soul level, to put up with so much of your stink.

Ah yes, it is perhaps the greatest gift one person can give to another is to give them an awareness of what they need for their growth, and allow them the space and freedom—the acceptance—to do it.

Laws:
8   The world is not "out there"—it is "in here."
10   The purpose of life is for those lessons.
18   Soul to soul pacts are made in the pre-existence:
33   Everything that happens in your life, happens for your highest good.
34   The heart wants what the heart wants.

Questions:
- Did you ever have a person such as described, come into your life?
- Are they still there?
- If not—how long did you allow them to stay?
- Do you appreciate the true gift they are gave to you?
- *Write about it.*

Of Controlling Women— and Scars

When I was four, I didn't seem to have good aim. My mother wanted to make a straight shooter out of me—and had me circumcised.

My first wife—she wanted to keep me on the straight by cutting off my balls every month or so with the sharp-edged threat of divorce. Yes, I gave her the control—Uh-huh! I begged.

Controlling women and scars . . . What's it all about for men? One left a little scar around my dick—the other, a great gaping picked-over scab across my heart, that seemed to take forever to heal.

So . . . a thought for the woman who feels she has a need to control. Don't you know that demanding a man be other than he is, gives one clear inescapable message:

> "I don't accept you! You are NOT good enough for me."

Now—assuming he loves you—that just has to cut deeply! Doesn't it just break your heart to know:

> *a scar is the most—and very best—*
> *you will ever give your man?*

The scary thing is: It is the same in everyone's relationships—man or woman. And the healing does not come from the one who controls. The healing must come from the love one holds for them self , body and soul.

The REALLY scary thing: not so many folks have that. For when one gives away control, one also gives away that self respect—that esteem one holds for one's self—and the controlling one, is who takes it away.

Is YOUR relationship built on control?

If there is that struggle, then there is but one way to stop it: STOP PLAYING YOUR PART—your part of the struggle and your part of the resistance to their struggle. Struggles usually start over the small shit anyway. And your feelings about the small shit are easily flushed.

Control is NEVER about love. By stopping the struggle you will find there is now room for love. Yet to stop the struggle requires courage. You may find that the person you love has not the ability to love back. Their relationships have only been about a struggle to control. Just know that to stop playing your part ONLY gives them the OPPORTUNITY to love—and love, is something they likely have never known.

Love is the gift you will then have to give—yes, takes courage when you know; it is a gift they may never accept. And, you may need to find someone who will.

This is not about me, preaching my beliefs. It is something I know from experience.

——— — — — ———

Laws:
2 Thoughts create.
8 The world is not "out there"—it is "in here."
16 Controlling anything outside ourselves is a fallacy.
21 Real love, once given, cannot be taken back.
28 Those times when life is at its most chaotic, are the times of most opportunity.

Questions:
- We have no right to change anyone's life except our own. Is there someone you are trying to change?
- Are you trying to make someone love you?
- Wouldn't you rather move on and find someone you can love, and who will love you back?
- Yeah, walking away is kinda like slogging through deep mud. But staying? That is asking someone to give you what they don't have to give?
- And you gotta have a clue by now that it isn't mud you're slogging through: it's shit—your own shit. *Write about it.*

Control is a Fallacy

Control . . .

Truth is, even those who were super achievers in control have only been but a fart in the vast universe of life. Some even lit the match to it all—Hitler, Stalin, Pol Pot, Kim Il Sung . . . They pretty effectively burnt their own asses, while leaving nothing but a bad odor behind as they left this world.

The truth of control is that you get to control another person's actions only to the extent that they will let you. And their thoughts—C'mon. You can shovel your shit into their minds only until they decide to think for themselves. Their hearts?—You get to control their hearts only so long as their experience of you feels good. For the average control freak—that won't be for long.

Control is something you can only do with yourself.

Laws:
16   Controlling anything outside ourselves is a fallacy.
13   Our life is our sole possession—and so it is for everyone.
15   To create a functional life requires one to do one's own thinking.

Questions:
- Do you know that so long as you are holding someone else responsible for your own feelings, you will have a need to control that person?
- And that should that person be your significant other, your relationship will be about control, instead of love?
- Can you see how your life will never be functional while you are breaking Law #13—or any of the Laws?

Change Is Scary

Yeah, I'm scared. My whole love life has been but a practice to this next relationship. I'm clear that it will all change. Change is always what is most scary—y'know? People will accept the most painful shit from the most overbearing of lovers just because it is familiar. Wanna know how scary change is?—Just look at what a battered woman will put up with, just to avoid change.

For me, since facing the imminence of my death I have not been accused of lacking the courage to face change. But then for me, what change could I face that is more dramatic than the one almost brought about by the Grim Reaper?

So . . . what do I know? I am not a battered woman facing death from a loved one rather than facing change—Or facing the truth that the one she loves, does not love her.

Yup! Facing the truth in our lives always means facing change.

The Grim Reaper brought truth to my life—and then change. But wait! The truth I faced was that the one I loved, did not love me and often threatened divorce. Emotional battery—physical battery? They're both battery, just not the same. But the truth?— They both leave bruises, they both leave scars! Perhaps I do know a little something. . . .

Laws:
14   Change is the constant of the universe.
21   Real love, once given, cannot be taken back:
9   Others are but a mirror for us to see ourselves.

Questions:
- Do you love someone who doesn't love you back?
- Do you know that you can leave them, and it is okay—the only real change for you, will be that you just won't have the drama of trying to make them love you?
- Oh, and if they are abusing you, you will be depriving them of their pleasure. Is that okay?
- Will you need to seek help to leave safely?

Trust a Snake?

A snake may change its scales, but it's always going to wear them. All you need determine is: Is it poisonous? Evolution with a real snake is not-so-much in question. It is a known fact that some snakes at some stage in evolution, once had legs.

Some people are analogized to snakes. Seems the same issues apply: Did they evolve, or devolve? Are they poisonous?

Is there any truth in the cautionary analogy—in the word "snake?" Was it passed on by someone's, possibly inaccurate judgment? Was it meant to keep you safe? Or to make themselves "right." Maybe that question needs to be asked, of both—and answered from beyond striking distance, of both.

Or maybe it is you, being called a snake to others. . . .

Laws:
3   Thoughts are energy.
15   To create a functional life requires one to do one's own thinking.
32   There is no good or bad, right or wrong, it is all God.

Questions:
- Most people are too lazy to think for themselves. Are you?
- Have you ever known someone to be called a snake, then it turned out not to be true? Was it you?
- People **ARE NOT** snakes y'know. Unlike snakes, people can change their minds. Did you, or someone you know change their mind?
- Was it, in fact, BECAUSE you changed your mind that you were/are called a snake? *Write about that.*
- **THAT,** is certain to result from every pious judgmental "friend" you ever knew, when you change your thinking to New Thought. You can regard this as a *cost* or a *gift—choose.*

Commitment is a Fallacy

Commitment . . . I think one only needs be committed to accepting the other person for exactly who they are without trying to change them. That is what makes a relationship safe for one another.

Marriage promises, and other legal agreements—those are the chains most view as meaning commitment. Truth is: there is no real security in that shit. It is a fallacy of an even magnitude with the one that says one person can control another. And in fact, it exemplifies two people in the act of attempting just that.

Commitment is a personal thing: something you make to yourself.

Laws:
21   Real love, once given, cannot be taken back.
13   Our life is our sole possession—and so it is for everyone.

Questions:
- **Doesn't requiring someone's promise to love you, act as a cock-block to real love?**
- **Can your love for someone ever guarantee you will want to be with them if your life together no longer works?**
- **Would you ever want someone to be with you only because they promised to be?**
- **Or would you rather know they are with you ONLY because they want to be?**

>>><<<

PART FOUR

Sex

More Than Inches

Just as it takes more than inches to make good sex,
it takes more than years to make one old.

Kinda comforting to contemplate
as I watch the years inch by.

Makes me wonder if on the yardstick of good sex,
my years rate any longer than my inches?

Now that would be a hard-won victory,
notwithstanding how hard it used to be. . . .

Laws:
8   The world is not "out there"—it is "in here."
17   The energy to which we hold fast is what runs our life.

Questions:
- What are you getting from this one?
- Are you thinking I'm just an old guy complaining about my short, soft dick?
- Or do you see me as an old guy comfortable with who he is?
- Do you see that perception IS a choice?

By the Cock

Ever heard a woman remark how men are led by their dicks, like it is the place where he keeps his brain.

I don't understand why they are complaining—Seems to me that there are a lot of ladies who control their men by using his cock as a leash?

Laws:
8   The world is not "out there"—it is "in here."

Questions:
Again, seems perception IS a choice. What do you think? *Write—*

>>><<<

"O" as in mOan

Most women spend a great deal of time blaming their men for all their pain—even though their pain is actually just a side effect of their thinking.

Well, except maybe for that part—that pain—which they welcome. That part is when—and if—he can change what normally looks like a "Y" to what looks like an "O." That's when the pain sounds more like the "O" . . . as in mOan!

Laws:
7 Along with being the creator comes responsibility.
17 The energy to which we hold fast is what runs our life.
8 The world is not "out there"—it is "in here."

Questions:
- To the ladies reading this: Did you take offense to this one?
- Does that place you in the category of the first paragraph, or the second? *Yup—write about it.*

Garden Hose Sex

Sex. . . .

Sex is like dealing with a cheap garden hose: Ya gotta work out all the kinks before you can get much flow going.

Laws—Questions:
Not touching this one with any length pole.

>>><<<

E-gasms

I think the best sex requires an element of love.

But let's face it, with many men, it is not their soul, not their heart, not even their dicks, but their ego, which does their fucking. I believe it is always so, until one learns how to love, and to make love. Until then, sex is just an orgasm of the ego—an E-gasm.

Problem with E-gasms? We men are the ones who slime ourselves—and no quick swallow is going to clean up that mess.

Laws:
3   Thoughts are energy.
4   The energy out, returns in kind.
9   Others are but a mirror for us to see ourselves.

Questions:
- Can you see how having E-gasms are about shoring up a sagging ego—a sagging sense of one's manhood?
- Do you think it works the same for a woman's ego?
- Is it about working our way/growing beyond the E-gasm, to the loving orgasm?
- Is that about taking it from a sense of self (singular) to a sense of selves (plural)?
- Are E-gasms necessarily a bad/unhealthy thing? *Write about it.*

Experiential Learning

The highest and best of learning, is obtained through experience—especially so, when learning about sex. Sometimes it takes experiential learning—and a pack of condoms.

Sometimes one learns all he needs to know, before getting to the condoms—sometimes not. That is determined by which head does his thinking, and whether her thinking matches his own.

Making love, or fucking—it all starts in the mind. The determining factor is which energy is expressed—love or fear.

Laws:
2   Thoughts create.
3   Thoughts are energy.
8   The world is not "out there"—it is "in here."
4   The energy out, returns in kind.

Questions:
- There is *making love* and then there is *fucking*. Which do you do?
- Do you have one of those rare relationships where you both do both?
- Or do you *make love* with one person and you *fuck* with another?
- However it is, are you honest?
- If your partner doesn't know how it is with you, do you have the courage to discuss it? (You either *do* or you *don't* there is no *can't*).
- If you think you *can't,* then which is it about: cowardice or lack of trust?
- You either are compatible or not. And sometime with such a discussion you become compatible. *What do you think? Write—*

Society, Sex, & Racial Inequality

This book asks you to let go of a lot of those rules of society, religion, and parenting. It's all stuff that has been ingrained into us from birth. All of it was aimed at making us think like they do—be, who they are. And maybe it is time to look at how dysfunction *they* are. Let's start with racial inequality and sex.

In the political climate of late, race has become a political weapon often wielded against the side that is not at fault by the side that is. What can I say that won't shock you? But then this whole book may come as a shock for a lot of folks, so why hold back now?

The whole race issue as it stands, cannot be explained as anything other than FUCKED UP.

But wait . . . maybe that is the answer—FUCKING.

With few exceptions, Man/Womankind are not color blind and we seem unable to "make it so." Despite any orders from our society, our religions, our families, even Captain Picard.

So let's take it to love—but first, let's not. So far, love has been unable to solve this problem. And maybe that is the answer: babies don't necessary come from love–or even from loving.

> *Babies come from FUCKING—*
> *and babies carry the DNA*
> *of the procreating races.*

Why not make it an issue for government to solve. What if they were to pass a law that you had to have your babies by someone of another race/color? What if they required you to be sterile when not ovulating and being inseminated—naturally or not—by a person of another color? If we did this, eventually everyone would be the same color—right?

Yeah, that might work—except for your partner's ego. Could he be man enough to accept that child just because it is YOUR child—and because the government says he *should?*. Few men would.

So okay—throw him in jail if he is a color-phobic racist. But wait! What about our freedoms—our inalienable rights? What about our whole, fucking, way of life?

Question is: would you be open to such stupidity? Seems it is the way our government is headed—and likely will go—should the power hungry side get their way. *But hey . . . I'm just a redneck patriot.*

Maybe the answer IS love. If you, as parents, started teaching your children to love, then future generations would eventually be all about loving or not? The issue would no longer be about the color of one's skin.

——— — — — ———

Laws:
3   Thoughts are energy—love or fear.
33   Everything that happens in your life, happens for your highest good.
5   The Universe always balances.
15   To create a functional life requires one to do one's own thinking.

Questions:
> Did you get a chuckle out of this whole wacked-out suggestion?
> ***It IS wacked-out****, do you think—**or not?***
> Could making everyone the same color actually be the way to go?
> Would this racist issue be worth giving up your freedom?
> Can government EVER really control what you think?
> Thoughts create—**YES!** Can you see how people do take their perception and make it reality?
> What if this insanely unworkable suggestion were the only solution? How fucked-up would that be?

Sex & Judgments

Most people put themselves into only one of the main categories—*straight, gay, or bi*. As with everything else in life, *labels* are a disservice. *They always* serve to limit one's self or others—as *judgments always do*.

Where sex is concerned, I don't label myself. And you? If you must, just label me *kinky*. Kinky is another word for *unlimited*.

Oh, there are things I don't have to try to know they don't work for me—the energy things—things that are sadistic, or demeaning.

Or things that strike me as goofy—not reality, not my reality at least. Things like furries—as in, you've gotta wear a *furry* costume. Real live furry? Now, that would be a kinky stretch—one where a lot of folks would get out their judgments. Would you?

--- --- --- --- ---

Laws:
8	The world is not "out there"—it is "in here."
3	Thoughts are energy.
15	To create a functional life requires one to do one's own thinking.
27	Life—all of it—is a spiritual experience.
32	There is no good or bad, right or wrong, it is all God.

Exercises:
- ➢ There are a lot of things that could be asked here. Sex is where a lot of folks' thinking gets judgmental. *Write about your own judgments.*
- ➢ While you are at it, *write about any judgments you may have about me for what I said here.*
- ➢ Speaking sexually, is it a stretch for you to accept the truth of law #32 here? *Why?*

Puberty

All children given time, will grow. Some even six inches at a time, and sometimes, multiple times a day. Such fluctuation for a boy is usually called "puberty." Ah, it is a wondrous time in life, just being a boy.

Laws:
1   I am the Creator.
2   Thoughts create.

Questions:
Have you reached your second puberty yet?

>>><<<

A Truly Selfish Mistress

I do my life to suit me. That you regard that fact as "selfish" does not concern me. Expecting me to live my life to suit yours is something I regard as being truly "selfish." But then, it is not my business to insist you see it my way. That is, unless I too, am selfish.

If what I do is physically harmful to you, tell me. I will jump through my own hoops to do it differently. But if what I do is just sand down your emotional pants—and you don't want to see it otherwise—then there is nothing left for me to say. Well, except maybe "Not being around me, for you, might just be better than diaper rash cream . . ."

Laws:
13   Our life is our sole possession—and so it is for everyone.
3   Thoughts are energy.
26   Change requires truth.

Questions:
- Change you, to suit them—can you see how this is one of society's nastiest lies?
- It is an impossibility (Law#26) unless you too want to change. Do you see, it is just a pretense that society demands?
- Kind of like you're masturbating the feelings of others to suite "society," don't you think?
- Is that okay with you—is there an orgasm in there anywhere for you?
- Yeah, society is such a selfish mistress—well, isn't she?
- Yes, I realize this is just such a machismo viewpoint—or is it?

Willing to Die For

Y'know, there really isn't any such thing as safe sex these days. Bacteria and especially viruses are pretty damn small things and can easily get through most any break in the skin—or the latex.

And during sex?—Well, those bodily fluids just naturally want to get exchanged.

For me, meaningless sex would only be fun if I were into playing Russian Roulette...

Guess what I'm saying is that I generally stay at home having safe sex with my rubber glove. Oh! That is, unless—as happens only rarely—I meet a women I'd be willing to die for.

So here is what such a woman—were she "perfect"—would be like:

> Gotta be pretty—to me.
> Chunky monkey or skinny minnie, she's gotta be fit.
> She's gotta be authentic—honest—no facade—WYSIWYG.
> Must love motorcycles, and dogs.
> And most of all, she must cherish me—without change—exactly as I am.
> Must appreciate a man with a crude sense of humor.
> Share a similar thought system—New Age—New Thought—"Conscious"—She's gotta understand me.

Oh, and yeah: I'm still single—

Hmmmmm....

Laws:
35   We have absolute abundance, limited only by our belief in ourselves—in who we are—as God.

Questions:
- Can you see how this law is exactly so—how I am guilty of breaking it?
- My relationships have always ended with me being rejected.
- Do you see what a magnificent creator I am in my life—how going into each one with that expectation has ALWAYS created just that result?
- No more! I see the truth in Law #35. I declare here and now in this writing—I await my soul mate's pleasure. Are you the one?

Man's Man vs. Gurley Man

How do women really want their men to show up sexually?

Maybe like the "Man's Man?" Like the guy from the power company who drills big holes to stuff big poles, ties them down with control wires, strings as many together as he can, them zaps them with as much juice as they will carry. Yeah, a real "Man's Man" has just gotta have a big dick!

But where does that leave me? Non-controlling . . . Certainly not a "Man's Man" . . . In the dick department, I'm pretty-much average. And yet, I am NOT an average man. Hell, to tell the truth, sexually I'm more like a lesbian on steroids, born in an average man's body. Do you suppose Arnold would call me, "a Gurley Man?"

And the ladies? If they really knew the way of it before the act . . . Would they choose the "Man's Man, or the "Gurley Man?"

Hell, I guess that is a choice only a woman can know and each must make . . .

---— — — ---

Laws:
34   The heart wants what the heart wants.
26   Change requires truth.
8   The world is not "out there"—it is "in here."

Questions:
- ➢ Am I making that choice any easier for you my love?
- ➢ Is anyone else reading this, "in here" with me? Creating begins with a thought, then speaking, then doing. We are talking about the ***doing*** part here. Is there anyone else ***doing*** this one besides me? *Writing is doing.*

PART FIVE

*Religion & God—
The Higher Power*

NOTE:

There are some very loving people in the many "organized religion" teachings—to include many of the officials of those various churches. When it comes to God very few folks would even dream of not taking what they're being taught as the "gospel truth."

Unfortunately it has always been so—

Given it comes from someone we know and respect, few people ever do their own thinking. That is EXACTLY what this book is asking you to do. Just because I say these things, and they are in a book, that does NOT mean they are gospel.

If you are a "religious" person, the things in this next section are likely to piss you off. That is because you will either see the truth and want to blame me for saying it—
AND/OR
Because you will realize that "religion" is another word for "indoctrination." You have been taught to see God in a way that allows the men/women of religion to use God as the sword of control over your entire life.

**DON'T CONTINUE READING THIS IF YOU ARE NOT PREPARED FOR THE TRUTH—
AND IF YOU DON'T WANT TO BE PISSED OFF.**

So to repeat:

> *When taking offense over something that is only about our own poor choice of feelings, we ALWAYS make ourselves a victim. BUT when it involves something that actually IS physically harmful to our lives, NOT taking offense ALSO results in us being a victim.*

Government and/or organized religions are heavy hitters. Barring armed rebellion, the ONLY thing we can do to resist is to SQUEAL LIKE A HOG as loudly and obnoxiously as possible. Others hearing will then take up the resistance. Only in this way will NONE of us be victims.

I said this same thing in a reflection titled *Repeating History*, in Book Two where I bitch-slapped (no offense meant ladies) the shit out of both government and Organized Religion—things over which we—us common rednecks individually—have little or no direct control.

Governments come and go, but "Organized Religion" has been KILLING untold millions for centuries. So if this following section seems a little over the top,

I SUGGEST YOU LISTEN-UP.

This is me

SQUEALING LIKE A HOG !!!

Backing Up

The following concept was covered previously, In case you missed it, it bears repeating now in a slightly different way.

There is no right or wrong—
There is no good or bad—
There is nothing sinful or saintly—

EXCEPT IN THE MIND!

They are JUDGMENTS that we make—God does not judge. God just loves. Religions judge in the name of God.

THE TRUTH IS: THERE IS ONLY LOVING OR UNLOVING.

Still that part of us that is not consciously connecter to God—that is NOT loving—has leeway to screw "love" around to mean anything that your devious purpose needs it to be.

BUT YOU KNOW THE TRUTH IN YOUR HEART.

And your heart is where the intelligence of emotion resides—your loving connection to God. Your spiritual growth centers around you discovering and connecting yourself consciously to that truth—to God. The more you do, the more "devious" is replaced by love—real love—God's love.

——— — — — ———

Laws:

3	Thoughts are energy.
8	The world is not "out there"—it is "in here."
32	There is no good or bad, right or wrong, it is all God.
33	Everything that happens in your life, happens for your highest good.

Questions/Exercises:

- ➤ Go back and re-read the long versions of each of the above laws. You may need do this exercise more than once before you can understand how they apply to the above.
- ➤ Regard this exercise as a tipping point to all you may ever discover about spirituality.. Don't stop until you are satisfied that you fully understand.
- ➤ Now assume that you have missed something and come back and do this exercise again after you have finished this book.

Jesus Died—

Jesus did not die for our sins, as religions demand that you believe.

"Sin" is just the *judgment* of man/womankind—as he/she was told to see it by religion. "Sin" is the bastard child of religion. Jesus died for the "sins" that the prevailing religious leaders of the time, judged him as being guilty of. Was he guilty—YES! He was guilty of telling the truth.

So . . . did Jesus die for our sins? NO. Jesus died that we might see who really wields the sword of judgment. YES, Jesus ABSOLUTELY died for us, that we might see, and rid ourselves of this thing called, "Organized Religion"—the thing that killed him.

I am NO Jesus! AND my bowels feel weak just contemplating my part in repeating his message—here and now. You may be assured that organized religion will try to crucify me also. Perhaps in the grace of the truth of God, the time has come for you to hear Jesus' true message.

IT HAS ALWAYS BEEN RIGHT THERE, FOR YOU TO SEE. I am NOT the only person with eyes.

Laws:
1   I am the Creator.
7   Along with being the creator comes responsibility.

Exercise/&Question:
> The thought that Jesus died for our sins is one held to be perhaps the most sacrosanct of all—not to be questioned, **EVER**.

> **QUESTION IT.** *It is the underlying lie that religions rely on to control you—that your salvation depends on Jesus, through them. Write—*

> Can you see that in one stroke, it releases you of all responsibility in the creation of your life, and lays that responsibility on Jesus—while binding you to that religion? Kind of a shitty thing to do to perhaps the greatest teacher of all time. He was probably the **ONLY** one who ever **FULLY** "knew" the truth of Law #1—a truth he referred to as a mustard seed. *Think about that—write.*

Suckling at the Cock of Religion

Yes, like most others, I too, went to the church of my parent's choice.

There, on my knees, I too, suckled at the cock of religion. And, as always, there were those "men of God"—preachers—speaking through their egos. Some must have gotten quite an orgasm out of my apparent servitude.

Me . . . now? These days I thank my indomitable soul that I did not swallow.

Jesus said it all well. But his words have since fallen in silence on the ears of those deafened by "religion" and "religious men of God" who would only use his words as whips for those chained and controlled by religion.

Now freed of the chains . . .
Those defining chains of all religions . . .
Those chains which would define and limit God . . .
Omnipotent—omnipresent—omniscient . . . God!
Yes, all powerful—all knowing—every-when—everywhere—within everything . . . GOD!

Yes, I see God, and he is all that—even to being within me—EVEN TO BEING ME! God cannot be within me, a part of me, without me also being a part of Him. Just so, IT IS THE SAME WITH YOU.

As to all the power that I will accept in the creation of my life—this man, this part of God that I am—even still, I hide from it all behind the shield of my own ego, my sense of self.

Do you get what a scary thing it is to know your real potential and fear all that you can be, were you to accept being that part of God who you are?

It would be so much easier to go back to church and just suck the cock of "Organized Religion." To believe they are feeding me God—one gob of splooge at a time.

But no. I'm not being homophobic when I say, "That just isn't who I am." Nor am I saying it is you. I'm just questioning: Is it true? Isn't that what organized religions do?

——— — — — ———

Laws:
All of them apply here. I expect some will want to crucify me for saying this in such an obnoxious manner.

Questions:
- Heavy handed? Yes. But not near so heavy handed as "Organized Religion," as STILL, it whips the power of God across the backs of parishioners. Have you broken free, or do you not notice the bite of the whip?
- Do you still believe in organized religion—that it is your connection to God?
- Or does that organized religion stand in your way—between you and God?
- Between you, taking back the power that was always yours?
- Heavy handed—obnoxious? Don't you think this is how you needed it to be?
- Can you hear me squealing, now?

Organized Religion

I was raised Mormon—but like I said, I just never swallowed. Once I got to a place where I started to think for myself, I looked at Mormonism. And I also looked around at the other religions. It didn't take long to come to some very clear realizations.

Me? Here are the questions I asked in coming along the way:

How much do organized religions have to do with actually worshiping God—or Allah, or whatever the Higher Power? And how much do they have to do with a man, or woman, wielding a sword called "God" to tell others what to believe, and how to live their lives to suit, and be controlled by themselves—threatening to cut you off if you don't submit.

Sword, or just a whip, on the one hand religion is about control. And on the other?—Well, you probably won't see much of the other. It is buried too deeply in your pocket.

And God?—that all-powerful being . . .
It is easy to see how some weak-willed person might want, even demand, our worship. And it is easy to see their greed for money. But God?—What kind of God would be so needy?

Laws:
ALL of them.

Questions:
- Knowing and believing these Spiritual Laws, this is what I believe. You? What do you believe?
- Given what the Bible says about God—Omni-everything—does it make sense to you that He/She/It would be so impotent as to make the demands they—"Organized Religions"—make on you in God's name?
- Speaking of the Christian Bible—you do know that it is a collection of early Christian writings—the ones that the Roman Emperor Constantine in 325 AD (Council of Nicea) decide was fit for you to know and believe in order to control the Christians, then—and still is controlling them today. You do know that, don't you?
- That is not to say that there is not great truth in the Bible—even truth that the Creator may have in some way given some of those writers to tell you. Do you see that I'm not questioning you or your beliefs in God?
- Who am I to tell you anything—has God inspired me? Look—I'm just following the rules of life—the ones that always hold true. And they tell me that "Organized Religion" has kept you on your knees for their own purposes—NOT God's. Can you accept that?
- Don't take my word for it—the LAST thing I want to do is tell you what to think. I am asking you to do your own thinking and then tell yourself. So, what DO YOU think?

One Heartbeat

Stupid shit happens and people die. Seems so tragic to us here in this existence. But is it tragic to the mind of God? He/She/It knows the pre-existence, this existence, and the existence that comes later. It is ALL existence to God. It is ALL God, isn't it? Is it possible that God sees this existence as the least loving overall? It's been said that if Humankind knew what the afterlife was like, we would all be dying to get there. Could that possibly be the truth?

Y'know, from our heart's first beat—sometime in the womb—to its last, we have always been just one heartbeat away from death. Maybe that last one is the best one.

And us? Aren't we a part of the energy—the essence—the actual reality of God? Aren't we like a drop in the ocean of God. If you've wrapped your mind around that one, then what is there to fear —or mourn—about death. Aren't we just mourning the fact that they are no longer here—but we are?

People do what people do. And shit happens—shit that on a conscious or unconscious level we have created.. We are the ones who choose how we look at it all—and, how we choose to feel. But God? God just experiences life through us. Just as God does, we also need to feel life from the pits of shittery to the heights of delight—OR none of it can mean shit. (Yes, this book is a real outhouse of information).

And we are the Creator—an actual part and piece of God. We choose the depths of our sorrow and despair—always. But then, we are still the Creator, we can then go out and find the ecstasy behind that experience. It IS there. The Universe—God—is always balanced.

Laws:

1	I am the Creator.
5	The Universe always balances.
8	The world is not "out there"—it is "in here."
20	God the Creator—that Higher Power—infuses the energy of the whole universe:
28	Those times when life is at its most chaotic, are the times of most opportunity.

Questions:
- No one gets through life without the wounds. *Write about yours.*
- Have you realized the great gift that was attached to each?
- Are you willing to search out the ones you haven't yet realized?
- Do you see how it is that to appreciate the sweet, it is necessary to experience the sour?

The "Wrath" of God

Many of the Christian sects teach about "The Wrath of God."

If you choose to look at that in light of the Spiritual Laws you'll realize, that it is fear based thinking—and unfortunately, is teaching you to think fearfully.

Spiritual Law states that there are only the two energies, remember: love and all that is not love (fear). It is not about me, making them "wrong," AND, don't you wonder why it is that fear, is what they would teach. Is this the truth of God—or is it another one of the lies of organized religion?

So what is it they are really teaching?

- God is a judgmental being.
- If you don't do as God (we) want, God will take revenge.
- If this is what God sees as being "right," then wouldn't God want us to emulate it? That is, to be judgmental and vengeful toward others?
- Is that a "loving" way to be? Wouldn't seem so, to me.
- How about you?
- So what that particular sect is really teaching is that God is only loving when you are doing what He (we) want.
- Some teach that God is a "Judgmental" god only.
- Others teach that He (I only say "He" because they also teach that God is a male) is both a "loving" God—when you do what He (we) wants, and a vengeful God when you don't.
- Loving—vengeful? Can you have both? Doesn't one deny the other?

Bottom line: they all demand that you live your life emulating God—don't they? And yet what they describe is nothing short of a dysfunctional God.

Yeah, I'd say that is a fitting description for a lie— DYSFUNCTION. Personally, I don't see that as a fitting description of God—do you?

─────   ─ ─ ─   ─────

Laws:
3	Thoughts are energy.
4	The energy out, returns in kind.
10	The purpose of life is for those lessons.
15	To create a functional life requires one to do one's own thinking.
32	There is no good or bad, right or wrong, it is all God.

Questions:
- How much of history has been colored by this dysfunctional teaching?
- How many nasty things has this organized religion teaching been responsible for?
- Has it also touched your own life? How?
- Did it cause you to be a mean, vengeful person—but in the name of God, of course?
- How'd that work for you? What did it cost you?
- Do you think living according to Spiritual Law is more functional? *Write about it.*

God Doesn't Do Diarrhea

If you're trying and trying, and what you want just ain't happening, then just let it go. When it comes to the Universe–to God, or however you look at that source to it all . . . When it comes to receiving the shit you want in life, God doesn't do diarrhea.

God gives you the shit you need, when you need it—big difference between want and need.

Laws:
35   We have absolute abundance, limited only by our belief in ourselves—in who we are—as God.
33   Everything that happens in your life, happens for your highest good.

Questions:
- If you have put your wants out to the Universe—to God—with intention and energy, then you have done your part. Do you know that?
- Are you now willing to get the fuck out of your way and let God do His/Her/Its job, in giving it to you—God's way?

PART SIX
Stray Thoughts

NOTE:

When I started putting this series together, I realized that those who do not already have a background understanding of New Thought would likely get lost very quickly. That is why I made it a workbook series.

Giving you these laws a few at a time and then laying out these thoughts—all designed to show you what the world looks like from their standpoint would serve to "show you" rather than to "tell you."

There are a lot of books that tell you about these laws. I don't know of any that are designed to show you.

Then I asked you questions to get you to thinking—some very pointed ones designed to take these laws to you personally. Of those who only read, and don't do the exercises or answer the questions, likely they only bought the one book and therefore are not reading this. With all this in mind here is the first of your final two exercises.

Exercise:
Read the 40 thoughts following and write down which laws they might represent. Then ask yourself how they might apply to your own life—specifically, what might they be saying about your thinking that needs to change for you to be who YOU want to be.

Stray Thoughts

Stray thoughts are like stray dogs: they come up to you in the oddest moments and lick your hand as if saying "Please—I just need someone to love me."

Perhaps you pet or caress them a time ot two, then walk on. Sometimes they follow you home and stay. And you end up loving them forever.

Love is like that. If it is given to you, it is nearly impossible not to receive it—and then to give it back. In that process a simple lick on the wrist can change your life completely.

Please accept the following stray thoughts of mine as a lick on your wrist.

Integrity vs. Morality

True integrity has nothing to do with morality. Integrity, remember, is when what one's heart feels, what one thinks/believes/says, and then what one does, all line up as the same thing. And has some essence of strength—of intention—holding it all together. True integrity is always only about *what is*.

Morality is only about someone's beliefs, their *judgments* of right and wrong. What is right and wrong exists only in one's own mind—and is never exactly the same in any other.

When you lay your morality as a condition to my integrity, there is not much I care to say about it. Except perhaps, that you are blowing your judgments out your ass, and it doesn't smell so good to anyone who is not judgmental like you.

Relax:
This is the last time you're going to feel this particular two by four up-side-your-head.

A Man Who Lies

A man who has to lie about what he's done in life?
Either he ain't done shit—Or, the shit he's done . . . really stinks!

Regardless, it is just his cry for love.

He doesn't see that you could ever love him without his facade of lies.

And you—are you still wearing your own facade?

Skid Marks

Everyone has acted like an ass at some time. Some act like one all the time. Showing one's dirty shorts is just part of one's personal growth.

So why fault them for it? Just remember that the skid marks they show today are the embarrassment that fuels their growth tomorrow.

Old Chinese Proverb?

What is most corrosive inside one's mind, cannot help but reek to the outside.

Pissing on Someone Else's Parade

Everyone's familiar with the old axiom for negative people who

> *". . . rain on someone else's parade."*

There are those who take it a step further. They think it's cute—those cartoons in the back of the old pick-up truck's window showing the mean looking little kid taking aim at "whatever" is the butt of the joke.

Well, maybe it's funny . . . Maybe it isn't . . . And, maybe the chuckles you get aren't about what you expect. After all, you see the kid. You see the stream. You see the intended butt of the joke. But that's about all. Maybe this is because, when you are busy pissing on someone else's parade, you cannot help but be exposing something very small about yourself to all who have the capacity to see beyond that butt. And it isn't necessarily that "something" one is holding in one's hand.

> *To see it . . . or not to see. Is there any question?*

About Psycho-babble

"Psycho-babble?"

Who, me?

Partner, don't you know that psycho-babble is just a term often used by them who're just too ashamed to face the truth about the tapeworms in their own shit?

What's that you say . . . "I'm challenging you?"

No. I'm not saying you're among such company—you did. After all, you did use of that term.

Oh, I see. You're offended by my choice of language?

Well, sure. I could have said it nicer—but then, would you have heard without use of the graphics? Sometime it takes the obnoxious to see your own obnoxcicities—yeah I know—that's not even a word. That happens a lot to those of us who like to babble. Y'know?

Taking Offense

When you take offense over your own unhappy feelings, you ALWAYS make yourself a victim. When you DON'T take offense when it is about something that affects your physical well-being, you ALSO make yourself a victim. (Yes, I've said this before).

Sticking you head in the sand and thinking only positive thoughts may be fine—for a while. But you've gotta realize that your butt is stuck up in the air, just ripe for the porking. And it won't be long before someone not-so-lovingly, will do just that.

I've noticed that with those who consider themselves to be "spiritual," many also consider themselves to be "liberal"—yeah, that whole left-wing socialist movement. Hell, it's been a disaster wherever it has happened throughout history. But that's what happens when your head's in the sand and your ass's in the air just waiting to be porked. . . .

For a while I figured they were mentally challenged. But that's not true. Simple truth is: Yup, you've got it—they've been PORKED.

Shit Happens

Shit happens—but always for a reason.
That being, that you have something to get clear *"on"*—or clear *"of"* in your life.

War of Words

To have a war of words, you need at least two combatants. If you only have one, all you have is an idiot standing there ranting and making an ass of him/herself.

Winds of Public Opinion

Think well before you try to piss on another person's integrity. The winds of public opinion could well end up blowing it into your face.

Male Maturity

I think the best indicator of maturity in a man is when he reaches that place in his life where he has plenty of testosterone with which to run his dick, yet has none left over for running his mouth.

It's My Shit— And, You Can't Have It

Yup, gotta admit: I've, stepped in my own shit more than once.

You know . . . That stuff you've got in your head that's all squishy and slippery—and it stinks so bad that you just don't want to even look at it. THAT kinda shit . . .

The only difference with me is that I won't blame my slipping and sliding stumbles in life on you. Rather, I will gladly own it, because that's the only way I can scrape it from my mind and the stench of it from my life forever.

He-e-e-re's Y'r Sign

Think about all the "fucked-up" people you've known in life . . .

But *own* this: "Fucked up" is just the sign you've put on them in your own mind. Y'might ask yourself: is it true? Or better . . . ask, what is true?

YES: they are certainly "fucked up—to *you*! But you can be certain that it is not so—for them.

For them—likely—the same sign hangs on you.
D'ya think maybe it's time to change y'r sign?

Add to Your Backbone

Was browsing through the online dating sites and came across one woman's profile. Didn't mean to be bickering with her—and, maybe I was. She wrote:

> " . . . I would like to meet someone that has not been emotionally, mentally and physically demolished by their past."

Here is my query to her:

> "Hmmm . . .
> You are a beautiful woman, and I liked your profile. AND, though I generally consider those who live that far away as 'unavailable,' the above statement really caught my eye. I have been there—done that—and consider myself so much better a man for it."

Not knocking your feelings, just wondering why you would not accept a man like me? I mean, if you're not a jellyfish, what doesn't kill you, likely will add to your backbone . . . dontcha think?

I received no answer—guess she just wasn't into hard-assed jellyfish .

Crazy Asses

There are a few crazy asses in this world who, when their needs aren't getting met—and/or they suddenly find themselves at odds with the rest of their world—will change themselves.

Been there—done that . . .

'Course this requires they first change something about their thinking. *No real change happens just by changing what one does—unless it is with an accompanying change in thinking. Until then life is just an act.*

The not-so-crazy asses—the *normal* folks—they expect the rest of the world to change to meet *their* needs. And, they will bounce off the walls until it does! Kinda makes their "act" turn into quite a drama.

Yep! Think I'll take my crazy ass and just keep on truckin'—

Fighting Over Shit

"There's some shit worth fighting over, and some that ain't." I know you've heard that saying.

Thing is, even when you win it's still shit, and it'll still stink . . . That is, if it was just shit to begin with.

Ever wonder if it really wasn't about the shit you were fighting over? Ever consider that maybe it was just about the win?

Whoa! Maybe you're just one of those folks who just has to have a bigger pile than everyone else.

But then, if that were so, wouldn't it just mean that you're the biggest asshole?

Me? I don't fight over any of that "shit." But rights and freedoms—

You don't want to try to stop me from standing-up for the American dream as explained in the Constitution—or from just being me.

Something Physical— Something Mental

Shit. Everybody does it. It is within all of us, both the physical, and the mental.

With the physical, only the smell of our own is acceptable to ourselves.

And the truth is, it is the same with the mental.

The next time you want to open up your mouth, you might pause to ask yourself if what you are about to say is going to be like a breath of spring air to others—sweet and uplifting—or something else.

That Is Unless . . .

Y'know, the feelings we have that don't feel so good? They're just there to point out our shit. And try as you might, you can't give 'em away—you OWN them—they're YOURS! That is unless . . .

Is it any wonder why most other folks dislike it so much when we are busy trying to wipe our feelings off on them. That is unless . . .

Yep! Y'got it: the "unless" is that you share the same shit. And the truth is, the only thing you give one another is a hand in ignoring that shit. And both your lives now stink twice as bad.

That is, to those who don't share that same shit.

Stinky Pants

Consider: If someone is wearing stinky pants, it just means they've worn them so long that they no longer notice the smell—but you do! Kinda begs the question: Are your own pants that stinky—or worse?

Suffering Fools

If you seek to make someone else out the fool—without even fully knowing for what they stand—then perhaps they are the one who is suffering the fool.

Waxing

Some people wax philosophical—some are merely crude. Perhaps both are communicating truth in their own way

.Me? I often wax philosophically crude.

Validating Stinkin' Thinkin'

Stinkin' thinkin' . . .

Yeah, it always seeks validation. After all, we know it is really all just our own personal mind shit.

If it were in your pants, the only way you could hide the truth would be by hanging around with others who smell just like you.

So too, stinkin' thinkin' requires the validation of like minds—dontcha think?

Doin' It

If you ain't doin' what you love . . .
You ain't living.

If you ain't doin' it with love . . .
You ain't loving.

And given, there are those who just ain't doin' it
Sad that their gift to this world . . .

Ain't anything anyone would want.
Everyone wants love.

Living the Truth

Those living a lie will unconsciously, seek validation.
Those living a lie consciously, will fight to the death for its truth.
Those living the truth don't give a rats ass what you believe.

Pink Paint

Does painting a turd with pink paint make it any more acceptable? Is it not still a turd? And what's wrong with turds anyway? Aren't they a necessary part of life?

Ah but with some, they seem to think pink paint disguises it. Kinda makes one wonder: how did they get that turd past that stick? If they had first removed the stick, would they then have felt a need for pink paint?

The Peanist

A person who plays with his penis is called a pervert. Is that because a person who plays the piano already has the title of "pianist?" And what about someone who likes to play the piano with one hand?

I dunno . . . but I'll bet it's a bitch to clean all those piano keys.

Stinky Shit

Shit only stinks when it ain't your own.

I think one of the secrets of true wisdom is in knowing just that—and that it is the same for all those other assholes as well.

'Course it helps to know that not all your shit comes out your ass. That which comes out of the bowels of your mind, can be the stinkiest of all.

Yeah, I know—'bout beat that point senseless here. But what I haven't mentioned is that either way—I think those who are wisest of all, do their shittin' in private.

So, please close the door and turn on that ventilation fan.

Thanks. . . .

The Direction It's Pointed

When your hormones groan and you're thinking with your little head, remember: It has no compassion. It will always want to move in the direction it's pointed—sometimes forward—sometimes back.

For something with such limited horizons, why is it so many women think it is that "little head" that does all of a man's thinking? Is she not being just as secular in her accepting.

About Honesty & Farts

Folks all claim they want honesty from you.

Truth is, honesty sometimes resembles a fart. You have a need to get it out, but no matter how you say it, it's gonna stink!

Question is, is it something they need to hear? And besides, could your "honest little fart" maybe have had a lump in it?—Can it possibly be your own shit that makes it stinks?

Sometimes honesty is best when expressed to your self —about your self—and in private.

Bickering

To me, "bickering" is when you unnecessarily stir shit up just to get the cesspool churning . . . y'know?
Me—I don't like the stink.

And I don't hang around with those who do—ya gotta wonder if it's just to mask the smell of who they are themselves. You know—kinda like politicians often do when they've done something particularly foul.

Dating—The Thrill of the Kill

For some, it is only the excitement of the hunt and the thrill of the kill. They've no interest in the care and preparation of the meat. Hell, they'd prefer to eat at someone else's banquet anyway.

I knew a woman like that—dumped me at the conquest and went back to her married lover. It's times like that when I really appreciate the perfection of life's lessons.

Going To the Dogs—

Back to those dogs—and their lack of sweat glands—how when they first meet they both smell one another's ass, in order to recognize each other in the future.

So . . . Why is it that we have so much trouble dealing with the stinking assholes in our own lives? Have they not also shown you the courtesy of knowing who they are for the future?

Take the High Road . . .

Most everyone knows what that is, and where it is. Still, so many get sucked under when trudging through the swamp—the cesspool of their ego—on their way to get there.

Ego Fucking

Sex is always the best when it is our hearts receiving the most enjoyment. Otherwise it is only about our ego getting its satisfaction.

Enjoyment of sex is multiplied by love. Yes, let's face it, with many men, it is not their soul, not their heart, not even their dicks, but their ego, which does their fucking.

I believe it is always so, until we learn how to love, and to make love—and that takes someone with heart.

Yes, this is almost a direct repeat. Something told me to leave it here—maybe that was just for you?

Sex For Barter

How many times has sex for me been about a means of barter, where either person was only doing it as a means of getting something else they wanted?

Seems so dishonest wouldn't you say. I can't know how it is in that other person's head, but in mine, I want sex to be a giving as much as a getting, but only for the purpose of sex itself.

I will never again knowingly fuck for anything other than the enjoyment of loving another person—and being loved back.

Move On

We all want to have things solid in our lives, just to have something to hang onto. Yet, the only solid thing about life, is ourselves–and those beliefs which serve us. As we grow and change, we come to realize how poorly some of those beliefs served—in fact, some never gave us any solid purchase in our lives.

When our beliefs begin stinkin,' it's time to let them go. Everything changes—it is the law of the Universe. I guess the trick is just to let those stinkin' things just slide away with their own flow.

Then as we gain a semblance of wisdom we start to realize that there are some things we can latch onto that do always hold true. Me? I found those things in the Spiritual Laws.

Have you taken a grip on these laws yet? I've thrown them out to you like a lifeline, just as they were once thrown to me. It's up to you to grasp them—or not.

I look back and am grateful that my life is no longer that whirlpool of dysfunction that threatened to drag me down to its stinkin' depths. But that was my life, have you looked at your own?

Y'gotta Know...

Shit's just a by-product of living. Without it you just wouldn't have life. Yet it is something we don't normally discuss in "polite society." And shit comes from both ends: the stuff that comes out of our minds, we generally don't discuss at all—unless it's to try to wipe it off on someone else with blame or for validation of its lies.

(I've run over that thought so much, it's now just a greasy spot on the highway. So enough—let's talk about the why).

Me? I prefer honesty. And I say *screw* "polite society!" It's not real—it's not honest.

Now take your family dog—true, honest, no deception, loyal, definitely real... Can't ask for a better companion—or teacher.

As mentioned previously, dogs don't have sweat glands. They familiarize themselves to one another by the smell of their butts. To them, shit's just a smell—not good—not bad—just is.

With us people, it is by the smell—or stink—of our minds by which we are known.

So with this book, y'gotta know: this old dog's just talking his shit. It is up to you whether this book represents a gourmets experience of exotic essences. Or if it simply stinks!

Yes, *perception is a choice.* And your perception here—your choice—is about you and your life. This book will tell you nothing, if it doesn't tell *you* about *you.* How you view everything, is what comprises your whole world—your whole life.

This book was deliberately written to be "in your face." Now you know why: and why this book can change your life—*if you want it to change.*

Yeah, honesty—naked vulnerability. How can I show you that in this book? It is what is necessary, if you want someone to know you, if you want to know that you are accepted—or not. And if you want to be of service to anyone facing the same issues in life.

Ed—It's My First Name

Y'know, I love going down to my local country saloon and two-steppin' to a country band. But right now my ankle is messed-up and I limp. That has only added to my appreciation of dancing. Hell, when dancing I don't even notice the pain.

Speaking of pain, I can only imagine what it is like for a woman who gets breast cancer and loses one or both breasts—gotta be painful, and it's gotta wreck her image of herself as a woman. That last part—that pain— I know well. Getting ED once wrecked my image of myself as a man.

Even with all this spirituality behind me—knowing that the mental pain is ALWAYS self created—I was devastated. Oh, I still had the "want to," but believed I needed to resign myself to never having another sexual relationship, ever again. Then a gal came along who wouldn't take "no" for an answer. She showed me how a male lesbian is actually preferable to many women.

Me? I can still orgasm. S'not so large, and not so hard—but it still worked. But that isn't what sex is about for me anymore. I suspect that the lesbian who takes the man's role, likely feels somewhat the same as I. What's most important to her, is her ability to satisfy the other—'course a macho redneck like me has no basis to speak for her. I only know, that's what it's about now, for me.

No. These days my dick is no longer big enough—or hard enough—to beat out massages like Tarzan on those jungle drums. But satisfying her added so much more to my image of being a man—and is so much more satisfying to me AS a man. And speaking "as a man" I am no longer sexually lame. I enjoy the dance with much more appreciation—and ability. I am no longer limping around on a crippled dick even though I still have ED.

Think about it. I'm longer constrained by man-meat—one size must fit all, and be hard enough, and last long enough . . . you get the point? She gets to have it any size, and texture, even augmented with its own built in vibrator. Strap it on and she can have it for as long as it takes.

Most men are mainly concerned with getting their own satisfaction—and in the process *some* will give the lady—hers. Ladies, if he's willing to face it honestly, a man with ED will always be bent on giving you yours. Given he has the "want to" and a open kinky mind, he can—and will—satisfy a like-minded woman, every time.

You know the old saying: When life gives you lemons. . . .
Hell, forget the lemonade. Make Kick-a-poo juice instead! Guaranteed to make your sexual adventures taste much better—

Oh, did I mention taste? I love the taste of my woman. So far, I've not found "the one"—I've no doubt, I soon will.

As for you other guys devastated by ED—it's said about 70% will be at some time in life—I hope I have served as an example of being—

- ➢ Being open-minded—
- ➢ Being authentic— I don't worry about what others think about me.
- ➢ Being someone who lives their truth—much more functional when you know the laws.
- ➢ Being someone who always chooses to live in the energy of love.
- ➢ Being someone with the courage to be "real." Yeah, I'm kinda beating on that "authentic" thing again. It does take courage.

When you care about the people in your life, then being willing to separate out those who don't care about you—yeah, that takes courage.

Another Personal Note

Undoubtedly, you've noticed that I cover the same concepts repeatedly. There is a reason—

Have you ever noticed that in commercial spiels, things are often repeated—sometimes in different ways, sometimes using exactly the same words. It is about setting it in your mind. They are trying to sell you something you may not actually want to buy.

It is the same here. There are things you don't want to hear because acknowledging them to yourselves will GUARANTEE that you will need to change something about your life.

And change is always scary.

So you try not to hear those things. Beyond repeating myself word-for-word, to get past your resistance what is required is to say it in some circumstance that is personal to your heart—something that reaches out and slaps you against the side of your head with a two-by-four of realization.

If I have gotten personal with even ONE such two-by-four here, then this book has been a catalyst of change in your life—and fuck all that boring shit it took to get you there.

Just a thought. . . .here is another.

Yes! I've laid some pretty horrendous stink on you with this book. That may well be what it takes for some folks to see their stick and to pull it out. You just can't get real if you've got a stick up your ass. That is what spirituality is all about—

Looking at your self with ABSOLUTE honesty.

You see, getting in touch with that higher power REQUIRES you to look within. YOU are an actual piece of God. If you want to know God, you 've GOT to start with knowing yourself—no matter how bad you may think you stink.

Try this:
The next time you're on the pot, before you flush, take a good look at that shit. Then with honest sincerity, thank it.

- ➢ Be grateful that it has been an enjoyable meal—
- ➢ Be grateful that it has nourished your body—
- ➢ Be grateful that it has given you the energy it takes to live and enjoy life—YOUR LIFE.
- ➢ Be grateful that it stinks—

And know this:
Again, you are an actual piece of God, the divine essence of the universe.

YOU ARE THE PART OF GOD THAT EXPERIENCES LIFE.

Then flush that shit and go find yourself a flower. Put it up to your face and breathe in the sweet fragrance of it. This can be the essence of your life here, to God.

Like that turd you flushed, you nourish God. When you live your life with joyful wonder, you are then like the essence of that flower to the divinity of God. You have to experience the stink to appreciate the flower. It is the same with God.

It's all good. It's all God—

AND YOU CAN BE THE FLOWER. . . .

PART SEVEN
The Final Exercise

Exercise:

If you have read even one of the three books (so far) in this series and done the work—if you have actually used a separate notebook to answer the questions and do the exercises—no doubt, your life has changed.

But it is not yet a done-deal. Nothing is ever done until you have taken it to "grateful"—and that's not to say you haven't already.

As a final exercise, write down everything that this book series has been the catalyst for changing in your life. Bless and be grateful to yourself for making those changes—DO THAT IN WRITING.

If you have been sitting in the bleachers reading this book then,

**GET YOUR ASS DOWN HERE ON THE FIELD—
AND DO IT!**
For your life to be in integrity, there is a part to it where you must "DO."
The doing part IS the journey of life—your life.

About the Author

I am a redneck. There are no academic accolades for me to brag about. Except for the fact that I am trained and certified by Coach University and did have a Personal Life Coaching practice for a time—but only a short time.

Putting myself in people's faces doing public speeches—constantly headhunting clients—didn't work for me. Even when I had enough clients, I could only influence their lives one mind at a time. With writing, I can do much more.

So, do I have any special abilities in writing? Even after all my warning, foul language and stink, you are still reading this, aren't you? In the other books I've written, the "About the Author" sections tell about me and my life to ad nauseam. I'm not going to do that here. Just know that **this book could never be written by anyone except a redneck.**

So . . . who'm I, that I dare say shit?

That I dare tell you anything about how life is?

Maybe I am nobody—maybe everybody. Certainly, I am no better than, nor much different from other men. Like them, I too have balls. Perhaps the only difference is—I'm letting you see mine.

That is because I don't give a shit how you see me. I have been to the brink of eternity—and returned. I know what matters in my life. And I know something about the lies I once believed, that did nothing but fuck that life up. That is what I know that might make me different from you.

I think one of the greatest truths of life is that we are all programmed by our maker to want our lives to count. The truth about the world is that we all do count. Many will leave a mark on history, but only a few will shine. Most are soon forgotten. Perhaps it is simply because most won't let others see the intimate parts we all think of as vulnerable—yes, I'm referring again to my balls.

Yeah, I've been kicked there. They did feel vulnerable. But is it possible to kick one's self there?

Yes . . . it is.

When I bow to my fears about what others will think—to my insecurities—it is then me doing the kicking.

Been there—done that—don't do it anymore.

If I did have any regrets about anything in these books, it would be that I did NOT treat organized religion or the left-wing of government with much love. Pointing out the truth of them was akin to bitch-slapping. (Again, just a redneck term—no offense meant, ladies).

And, maybe it was not-so-loving in that I know they won't like it, and, it is the truth. I hold them capable of facing the truth of what they do—it is not *who* they are, just *what* they do.

To remind you one last time:

> *By taking offense with things that don't affect your life physically—only your feelings—you are making yourself a victim. However, by NOT taking offense with things that ARE detrimental to your life physically, you also make yourself a victim.*

Why do you think it is that this has been repeated so often?

By trying to tearing down the Constitution, left wingers are actually threatening my freedom. Besides which they—in effect—are shitting on the grave of every dead soldier who ever fought and died for those freedoms.

Organized religion? No, it no longer affects my life physically—other than through the thousands of people dying needlessly in this world, right NOW, because of someone's thirst for power. With all organized religions there is a thirst for power, but currently, the worst offender would be extreme Islam.

The people themselves causing all this destruction?—Misguided or not, I can love them—we are all connected—but as for this book, all I can do is bitch slap them for what they do, by pointing out the bald-faced truth under spiritual law.

NOTES

NOTES

NOTES

NOTES

CPSIA information can be obtained
at www.ICGtesting.com
Printed in the USA
BVHW031604040219
539433BV00001B/118/P